Toward a Critical-Inclusive Assessment Practice for Library Instruction

Toward a Critical-Inclusive Assessment Practice for Library Instruction

Lyda Fontes McCartin and Rachel Dineen

Library Juice Press
Sacramento, CA

Copyright 2018 Lyda Fontes McCartin and Rachel Dineen

Published by Library Juice Press in 2018

Library Juice Press
PO Box 188784
Sacramento CA 95818

http://libraryjuicepress.com

Printed on acid-free paper.

Library of Congress Cataloging-in-Publication Data

Names: McCartin, Lyda, author. | Dineen, Rachel, author.
Title: Toward a critical-inclusive assessment practice for library
   instruction / Lyda McCartin and Rachel Dineen.
Description: Sacramento, CA : Library Juice Press, 2018. | Includes
   bibliographical references and index.
Identifiers: LCCN 2018027563 | ISBN 9781634000352 (alk. paper)
Subjects: LCSH: Library orientation for college students--Evaluation.
Classification: LCC Z711.25.C65 M37 2018 | DDC 025.5/677--dc23
LC record available at https://lccn.loc.gov/2018027563

TABLE OF CONTENTS

ACKNOWLEDGEMENTS

We wish to express our thanks to the people, places, and pets who helped make this book possible. The most important people to thank are our students—past, present, and future. They teach us every day and make us better. To Greeley, Colorado's Cranford Tea Tavern, Margie's Java Joint, Village Inn, and Rio—thank you for the comfortable seats, flowing caffeine, margaritas, wifi, and for never kicking us out! To our spouses, Charlie McCartin and Mark Dineen—thank you for your support, and for never telling us this was a bad idea (at least not out loud). Scotty, Moose, Cliff, and Chai—thank you for the licks and lap cuddles, your emotional support is invaluable. This book could not have been written without the help of Shannon Smith, a wonderful graduate assistant. The critical feedback from Benjamin Harris, Jennifer Foley, Jennifer Leffler, and Blake Carrey was crucial to getting this book done—thank you for not holding back! Alison Lewis—thank you for answering all of our questions and for being flexible about the due date. Dr. Chayla Haynes Davison—we would not have started these conversations with each other without your guidance; you'll never know how influential you've been! Finally, our amazing colleagues who supported us for the past year and a half, Brianne Markowski, Stephanie Evers, Darren Ilett, and Natasha Floersch—thank you for understanding when we moved meetings, for never telling us to shut up when we kept talking about our book, and for understanding our need to work away from the office. Your support for this endeavor means everything.

Foreword
Benjamin R. Harris

Critical librarianship and assessment of student learning and teacher performance should not fit together. In 2013 when I began work on a project with my colleague, Anne Jumonville Graf, on critical information literacy and library assessment, we believed that our article would dismantle some of the common ideas about assessing library instruction. Our contention would have been that thinking about critical librarianship and the vogue in assessment practice meant that you had to choose one or the other. You couldn't have both.

At that time, we imagined two distinct and disparate audiences: those interested in the critical side of our argument and those focused on assessment from conceptual to practical approaches. We did not believe that there would be much of an overlap in these two groups that had very different expectations and concerns. An early reviewer of our work confused critical practice with teaching critical thinking; another believed that a critique of the assessment conversation in our literature was a negative approach to change. Since that time and those discussions, we have seen our professional and scholarly conversations infused with Freire, bell hooks, and critlib hashtags, so I imagine a that a wide variety of readers may find their way to this text.

So, who are you? Specifically, I am thinking about the different reasons that you may have chosen to read this book offering a critical-inclusive perspective on assessment in libraries.

Are you just beginning your exploration of critical librarianship? If so, you are starting in an ideal place. Chapter One of this text offers a concise introduction to critical pedagogy that blends traditional sources with more recent voices and considers the key authors on this topic in the library literature. You will have a chance in later chapters to see how this pedagogy plays out in the praxis of the writers, who conscientiously detail the successes and challenges of this path.

Are you participating in the critical librarianship conversation? Are you interested to see the ways that assessment may be part of the project instead of apart from it? If you are skeptical at first, I am sure that you are not alone. It still feels like an uneasy fit. McCartin and Dineen embrace the uneasiness and deal with it directly, in ways that force us to question our critical practice and our assessment concepts and strategies so that we may better understand them. In thinking about it, there is a consistent process model throughout the text that could be summed up using these key actions: question, explore, understand, embrace.

The authors build upon our critical librarianship discussions as they integrate the work of Dr. Saran Stewart into their discussion of pedagogy and practice. This move is of great value to us as they bring Stewart's voice to our attention. While longstanding writers on critical topics continue to inform us (and should), the work and insights of current writers—navigating contemporary waters with a critical pedagogical lens—speak to the times and the context in which we currently act. The authors go a step further and interpret Stewart's work in direct relationship to the needs and interests exhibited in our discussions on assessment.

Are you primarily interested in assessment, and hope to see new approaches and ideas about telling your library's story? Using Stewart's critical pedagogy schema, the authors create a comprehensive vision for assessing library instruction. This is a model that should encourage a deep and connected understanding of the different types of assessment we can conduct and the ways they are related to each other and to larger individual, group, or institutional goals. This effort does not compromise or subvert assessment; rather, the authors enhance our understanding of the possibilities with their approach and application. Readers will be inspired to try some new strategies but, even better, we can all see anew those strategies that have become engrained or so familiar that we fail to note the potential of making adjustments—either in the strategies themselves or in our thinking about those strategies.

What readers of all intents will find thrilling in the following pages is the blend of considered, considerate thinking about critical librarianship and straightforward practical application. The writers pull no punches. A critical-inclusive assessment practice is not easy and in its own way may be painful at times—but worth it. The potential benefits turn the challenges into opportunities; the challenges themselves suggest the vitality of this project and the risks inherent in any path that is not yet cut. And along the way, we are introduced to two of our colleagues in the profession. This is not just a consequence of offering an applied account of critical librarianship at work in assessment practice, but also a conscious effort on the part of the authors to embody theory and experience for the reader. We grow with the writers as they explore the foundations of their experiments and examine the results of their efforts.

In thinking about possible audiences, I neglected a very important group. Maybe you are new to the profession or soon to graduate and you are interested in recent scholarship on teaching and learning (broadly, or in librarianship specifically). You arrive as a colleague at a nourishing, flourishing time, as we are seeing teaching, learning, patron development, and assessment with a fresh perspective on our influence and responsibility. You will find this to be true when you read this text. I hope you will see that, as we become seasoned librarians and information professionals, we are people who continue to question, explore, understand, and embrace.

Benjamin R. Harris
Professor
Elizabeth Huth Coates Library
Trinity University
San Antonio, Texas

PREFACE

As two librarians who believe strongly in the value of assessing student learning and the continuous assessment of our own teaching, we find a distinct gap in the critical information literacy (CIL) literature. Most librarians talking about critical practice are not talking about assessing learning. If it is discussed, librarians mention what could be done without providing examples of assessment in practice. Because of this gap in the literature, we decided to write a book combining our knowledge of assessment with our desire to engage in critical pedagogy. When we outlined this book for Library Juice Press in 2016, we planned to share practical approaches for creating democratic classroom spaces and discuss our experiences applying long-established assessment techniques re-envisioned through a critical lens. However, when we started preparing these new assessments and after reading critical pedagogues, especially those involved with assessment, we realized that simply re-envisioning established techniques wasn't really possible. Moving toward critical-inclusive assessment required a complete makeover of our existing assessment practice.

Since fall 2016, we've been changing our practice with a focus on democratic classroom spaces and moving toward a critical-inclusive pedagogy. We've restructured our credit courses, updated one-shot curriculum, incorporated peer review of teaching, and worked to involve students with assessment. We've had conversations with each other over the past year-and-a-half about authority vs. authoritarianism and our role in the classroom. This book is an illustration of our praxis. In it, you will find discussions regarding why we believe that critical-inclusive assessment practice can work. We are convinced that assessment has its place in our pedagogical practices and does not have to hinder our attempts to uphold critical, feminist, or inclusive ideals. We see an inherent similarity between critical information literacy and assessment in that they both support hope for the future and progress towards positive change. We hope this book will help other librarians engaged in critical practice to approach assessment in new ways by working with students as partners in curriculum development and fostering more democratic and inclusive classrooms.

Our Journey to Critical Practice

Similar to other librarians,[1] our paths to critical and inclusive pedagogical practices have been emotional. There are times when we feel empowered and excited to have engaging conversations in the classroom. There are times when we feel confused or overwhelmed by the task, and entirely inadequate to make any sort of real change. Then there are times when we are compelled to want to know more, to read everything we can, to experiment, to discuss, and to ask questions. The following passages briefly outline our individual journeys into critical practice and our collaborative journey to being more critical and inclusive pedagogues.

Lyda's Story

Theory wasn't a significant part of my undergraduate or graduate careers. As a history major, I spent a lot of time analyzing primary documents and thinking about why a particular event happened in a certain way or hoping to find an undiscovered record hidden deep inside an archive. I taught history as an adjunct at a university while I was in library school. Looking back, I realize that I wasn't a

---

1. Robert Schroeder, *Critical Journeys: How 14 Librarians Came to Embrace Critical Practice* (Sacramento, CA: Library Juice Press, 2014); Annie Downey, *Critical Information Literacy: Foundations, Inspiration, and Ideas* (Sacramento, CA: Library Juice Press, 2016).

great teacher during that time in my career— I would come in and give my lecture and students would listen, take tests and quizzes, write papers, and receive grades. It wasn't a particularly engaging space. In fact, I was quite bored teaching history, which is odd considering how much I love the subject. But I hadn't been taught how to teach, so I was flying blind and knew little about how to engage with students in the classroom.

When I began teaching in libraries, I was a graduate assistant and simply followed what my supervisors did. I would do a little bit of demo with a worksheet in most of my sessions. When I got my first job and started teaching my own credit courses and a large number of one-shots, I was still doing a lot of demonstration, but it didn't take long before I realized that students seemed to get a lot more out of the sessions if they had more hands-on time. As I began to add more and more hands-on time into my one-shots, the classroom environment changed; students were able to engage more with their own topics, and I was able to interact with students one-on-one. This meant that I could help advanced students get into different resources while helping others with the basics. I'm not the only librarian who came to this realization, of course, but this is when I started reading more about active learning. Sometimes I wish I could go back to that history classroom with the knowledge of teaching that I have now. It would be a different classroom, and I think my students would enjoy it.

I came to critical information literacy in 2016 by way of a doctoral course on culturally-responsive and transformative learning. In this course I was introduced to Paulo Freire, bell hooks, concepts of transformative and culturally responsive teaching, and inclusive classrooms. During this course I did a lot of self-reflection on my identities and privileges and how they influence the classroom and students. It was during this course that I found Maria Accardi's *Feminist Pedagogy for Library Instruction*[2] and Shana Higgins and Lua

---

2. Maria Accardi, *Feminist Pedagogy for Library Instruction* (Sacramento, CA: Library Juice Press, 2013).

Gregory's *Information Literacy and Social Justice*.[3] Finding these works, and others on social justice and libraries and on critical information literacy, led me deeper into critical theory to topics such as Critical Race Theory and Critical Race Feminism. One day in 2016, I walked into Rachel's office and found *Pedagogy of the Oppressed*[4] on her desk. I recommended that she read *Teaching to Transgress*,[5] and there began a collaboration to read, discuss, and learn from each other about reimagining our practice.

Rachel's Story

Shortly after graduate school, I began volunteering with an adult literacy program in Detroit. I entered into this opportunity thinking that I would be working closely with a student on a specific goal, like studying for and passing the GED exam or preparing for the U.S. citizenship test. I envisioned having a meaningful relationship with this student based on respect and shared learning goals. What I actually experienced, however, was far different. My student was assessed at a reading level of one, meaning we would be working on the very basics of reading and writing, relying heavily on the content provided by the program. He humored me as we read about a man with a pan, or the cat sitting on a mat. Even after our first few sessions, it was clear that we were both a little embarrassed and very bored. Lamenting the fact that "this was not what I signed up for," I contemplated quitting. I called my dad, a retired secondary teacher, for advice. He suggested that in our next session, we should just talk. What an incredible idea! While my student could not necessarily articulate learning goals, he could tell me what he liked. I learned that he liked to cook, listen to music, and play basketball. We ditched the workbook and began

---

3. Lua Gregory and Shana Higgins, *Information Literacy and Social Justice: Radical Professional Praxis* (Sacramento, CA: Library Juice Press, 2013).

4. Paulo Freire, *Pedagogy of the Oppressed*, New rev 20th-Anniversary ed. (New York: Continuum, 1993).

5. bell hooks, *Teaching to Transgress: Education as the Practice of Freedom* (New York: Routledge, 1994).

to develop our own curriculum, together, based on his interests. Although I didn't know it at the time, I was incorporating critical pedagogy into those tutoring sessions. It was the first time I began to appreciate the importance of student voice and experience in the classroom, and they continue to inform my pedagogical practices and research interests.

In early 2016 I started a new job that launched my journey to a more structured introduction to critical theory and critical information literacy. In Lyda, I found not only an encouraging mentor, but also a comrade in exploration of critically focused literature. We bonded over reading Freire's *Pedagogy of the Oppressed*,[6] and Accardi's *Feminist Pedagogy for Library Instruction*.[7] We discovered the discussions happening on Twitter under #critlib and we continue to read as much as we can find within the field of academic libraries and beyond. Any strategies for an inclusive classroom that I try, I first discuss with Lyda. This embedded support system has been developed through our shared interest in critical and inclusive pedagogies.

Where We Are Now

Although we have started to implement critical, feminist, and inclusive strategies into our information literacy classrooms, we struggle with calling ourselves critical or even feminist pedagogues, because we know that we are not always working toward breaking down systemic power structures or ending sexism and sexual oppression. If the true measure of the success of critical pedagogy is social change, then we can't identify as critical pedagogues because we are not activist scholars and we are not actively encouraging students to work for social change through our teaching. Yet, our work does create change—change in our teaching, improvement of our own pedagogy, and a change in our assumptions about teaching, learning, and our students.

6. Freire, *Pedagogy of the Oppressed*.

7. Accardi, *Feminist Pedagogy for Library Instruction*.

Implementing a true critical pedagogy in an information literacy one-shot session may not be possible.[8] Librarians interviewed for Annie Downey's 2016 work on critical information literacy "spoke at length about the impossibility of enacting critical pedagogy in university settings in general and library instruction classrooms in particular."[9] We thank Downey for listening to these critiques of critical pedagogy in library instruction and breaking apart critical methods from critical content:

> Critical pedagogy in its purest sense as it was understood and enacted by Paulo Freire and his followers would be next to impossible to pull off in library classrooms. The library profession, libraries, and colleges and universities present obstacles that while not entirely insurmountable, are big enough that they heavily impact librarians' freedom in the classroom. The teaching methods that critical pedagogy offers us, combined with the rich possibility offered by critical information literacy content, provides a set of ideas and concepts that librarians can use to make their information literacy work more critical, engaging, and meaningful. But when critical methods are not possible, critical content can help librarians get closer to meeting their teaching goals.[10]

Reading this, and the concerns of other librarians who work in critical practice, encourages us to keep moving forward.

Organization of the Book

In this book we present a detailed discussion about taking a critical approach to the assessment of both teaching and student learning. Each assessment technique discussed is a method that we have personally tried in our information literacy classrooms. By reading each chapter in order, you'll find the following:

- Foundations of our pedagogical practice

---

8. Downey, *Critical Information Literacy*, 105.

9. Downey, *Critical Information Literacy*, 105.

10. Downey, *Critical Information Literacy*, 106.

- An introduction to the Critical-Inclusive Pedagogical Framework
- A discussion of the approaches to critical assessment of teaching
- An historical survey of alternative methods of student-learning assessment
- Methods for assessing teaching practices
- Methods for assessing student learning
- Plans for future critical-inclusive assessment practices

In Chapter One, we present a conversation about the foundations of our pedagogical approach, including a discussion of critical pedagogy and critical information literacy. We introduce Dr. Saran Stewart's Critical-Inclusive Pedagogical Framework,[11] which provides a foundation for our practice. In Chapter Two, we offer a review of the current state of the literature on the assessment of teaching and learning. We discuss techniques for assessing teaching practices and then share an overview of alternative student-learning assessment methods, outlining techniques both inside and outside of libraries. In Chapter Three, we provide a discussion of techniques we use to assess our own teaching. These include peer observation, journaling, and Critical Friends Groups. We provide tried examples of these assessments, and offer suggestions based on our experiences. Chapter Four provides real-world examples of student learning assessments that stress student involvement and student voice. In that chapter we offer critical reflections on our work and recommendations for implementing these techniques. Finally, in Chapter Five, we outline our plans for the future and discuss how we continue to evolve our practice.

We hope that you enjoy this book and find it useful for your own practice. If you are picking up this book because you are skeptical about the relationship between critical practice and assessment,

---

11. Saran Stewart. "Advancing a Critical and Inclusive Praxis: Pedagogical Curriculum Innovations for Social Change in the Caribbean." in *Race, Equity and the Learning Environment: The Global Relevance of Critical and Inclusive Pedagogies in Higher Education*, ed. Frank Tuitt, Chayla Haynes, and Saran Stewart (Sterling, VA: Stylus Publishing, 2016), 9-22.

we ask that you keep an open mind. If you are picking up this book because you want to align critical practice and assessment, we encourage you to try these techniques and let us know how they work for you.

Lyda & Rachel
Greeley, Colorado
June 1, 2018

Chapter One

FOUNDATIONS OF OUR PEDAGOGICAL PRACTICE

It is important to remember that librarians are not teaching
information literacy. We are teaching people. Information
literacy is simply the means by which we teach people.[1] It is also
important to remember that we are teachers and learners and that
"we learn best when there is an interactive relationship between
student and teacher."[2] We are personally inspired by tenets of
feminist and inclusive pedagogies that work to deconstruct
traditional hierarchies in the classroom. Our aim is to improve
our teaching in increasingly diverse classrooms, ensuring that our
classrooms are places where all students can succeed.[3] Ultimately,
we want classrooms that foster fairness and equality, sustain an
environment of inclusivity and care, and promote mutual respect.
The following is a discussion of the theoretical and practical
foundations that center our teaching and assessment practice.

Critical Pedagogy

Critical pedagogy "seeks to use education to empower students
to overcome racial, class, or gender barriers that exist in society.

---

1. Michael Fielding, "Radical Collegiality: Affirming Teaching as an Inclusive Professional Practice," *Australian Educational Researcher* 26, no. 2 (1999): 1-34.

2. hooks, *Teaching to Transgress*, 19.

3. Frank Tuitt, Chayla Haynes, and Saran Stewart, *Race, Equity and the Learning Environment: The Global Relevance of Critical and Inclusive Pedagogies in Higher Education* (Sterling, VA: Stylus Publishing, 2016).

This approach seeks to turn education into a dialogue with students about the state of the world. The result of this dialogue is to enact change."[4] Paulo Freire introduced our current understanding of critical pedagogy in 1970 with the publication of his seminal work, *Pedagogy of the Oppressed*. In it, he describes the problematic mechanistic nature of education in which teachers "deposit" knowledge that students "patiently receive, memorize and repeat."[5] Rejection of this "banking" concept in education is the cornerstone of critical pedagogy. Since 1970, Freire has published numerous works that expand upon his thoughts on education.[6] Contributions to the theory of critical pedagogy have also been made by scholars and theorists who have built on Freire's work, including bell hooks, Peter McLaren, Henry Giroux, Ira Shor, and Joe Kincheloe.[7] According to McLaren, "critical pedagogy is a way of thinking about, negotiating, and transforming the relationship among classroom teaching, the production of knowledge, the institutional structures of the school, and the social and material relations of the wider community, school, nation, and state."[8] Giroux claimed that "it is best to think of critical pedagogy as an ongoing project instead of a fixed set of references or prescriptive set of practices, put bluntly, it is not a method."[9] Kincheloe notes, "critical pedagogy is a complex notion that asks much of the practitioners who embrace it," meaning that critical teachers must be dedicated

---

4. Troy Swanson, "Applying a Critical Pedagogical Perspective to Information Literacy Standards," *Community & Junior College Libraries* 12, no. 4 (2005): 66.

5. Freire, *Pedagogy of the Oppressed*, 53.

6. For more information on Freire and a bibliography of his work visit "Paulo Freire," *Internet Encyclopedia of Philosophy*, accessed May 30, 2018, https://www.iep.utm.edu/freire/.

7. Eamon Tewell, "A Decade of Critical Information Literacy: A Review of the Literature," *Communications in Information Literacy* 9, no. 1 (2015): 24-43.

8. Peter McLaren, "Che: The Pedagogy of Che Guevara: Critical Pedagogy and Globalization Thirty Years After Che." *Cultural Circles*, (1998, Summer), quoted in Joan Wink, *Critical Pedagogy: Notes from the Real World* (New York: Longman, 2000): 30.

9. José María Barroso Tristán, "Henry Giroux: The Necessity of Critical Pedagogy in Dark Times," *Truth Out*, February 6, 2013, para. 4, http://www.truth-out.org/news/item/14331-a-critical-interview-with-henry-giroux.

to "more than learning a few pedagogical techniques."[10] This is especially important for critically-minded librarians "since a significant amount of the pedagogical work we do happens outside of the traditional classroom setting."[11] For us, critical pedagogy requires dedication to flexible and responsive teaching, reflective practice, and engaging in dialogue.

Flexible & Responsive Teaching

A critically-minded teacher recognizes that students come to the classroom with their own knowledge, experience, and needs. Understanding the best ways to make use of those attributes requires an educator who is flexible and responsive. Whether it is changing lesson plans based on formative assessment or engaging in impromptu discussions to address the emotional state of the classroom, flexible and responsive teaching requires intuition and a bit of improvisation. Donald Schön defined the concept of reflection-in-action as it relates to the type of observation that happens simultaneously with events as they occur.[12] This type of reflection directly results in quick, responsive decision-making. Flexible and responsive teaching also requires courage. Having the confidence to stray from a thoughtful lesson plan is not an easy task; it can be viewed as failure. While most critically-minded teachers would agree that it is an important part of learning, failure is difficult to embrace. In an interview discussing the fear of failure, hooks remarked that "there are moments when I worry that I am not being a 'good' teacher, and then I find myself struggling to break with a good/bad binary. It's more useful for me to think

---

10. Joe Kincheloe, *Critical Pedagogy Primer,* 2nd ed. (New York: Peter Lang Publishing, 2004), 2.

11. Heidi Jacobs, "Information Literacy and Reflective Pedagogical Practice," *Journal of Academic Librarianship* 34, no 3 (2008): 257.

12. Jennifer York-Barr, William Sommers, Gail Ghere, and Jo Montie, *Reflective Practice to Improve Schools: An Action Guide for Educators* (Thousand Oaks, CA: Corwin Press, 2001): 4.

of myself as a progressive teacher who's willing to own both my successes and failures in the classroom."[13]

Reflective Practice

Expanding on Schön's concepts of reflection-in-action, we also see the significance of reflection-on-action, which refers to looking back at experiences as guideposts for future changes.[14] Reflection is many things. It is difficult; it is essential; it is time consuming; and it is impetus for change. There is an extensive literature on the value and necessity of reflection for teachers.[15] John Dewey saw reflection as "the intentional endeavor to discover *specific* connections between something which we do and the consequences which result, so that the two become continuous."[16] Critical self-reflection, or metacognition, is fundamental to critical information literacy and librarianship as a whole. This is evidenced by its inclusion in the *Framework for Information Literacy for Higher Education.*[17] As a necessary component of praxis, reflection plays a large role in our teaching.

Engaging in Dialogue

For hooks, "it is crucial that critical thinkers who want to change our teaching practices talk to one another, collaborate in a discussion that crosses boundaries and creates a space for interventions." hooks continues by saying that "dialogue is one

13. bell hooks, *Teaching to Transgress,* 158.

14. York-Barr et al., *Reflective Practice to Improve Schools,* 4.

15. John Dewey, *Democracy and Education: An Introduction to the Philosophy of Education* (New York: Macmillan, 1916); York-Barr et al., *Reflective Practice to Improve Schools;* Heidi Jacobs, "Information Literacy and Reflective Pedagogical Praxis"; Jennifer Moon, *A Handbook of Reflective and Experiential Learning: Theory and Practice* (New York: Routledge, 2004); and Maria T. Accardi and Michelle Reale, "Critical Reflection to Improve and Grow as Librarians Who Teach" (Webinar, June 2, 2017).

16. Dewey, *Democracy and Education,* 170.

17. Association of College and Research Libraries, "Framework for Information Literacy for Higher Education," adopted January 11, 2016, http://www.ala.org/acrl/standards/ilframework.

of the simplest ways we can begin as teachers, scholars, and critical thinkers to cross boundaries, the barriers that may or may not be erected by race, gender, class, professional standing, and a host of other differences."[18] Professional dialogue is definitely essential to our practice. We've spent many hours discussing and debating critical information literacy approaches, lesson plans, and assessments. Our department engages in bi-monthly theory meetings, which gives us the opportunity to talk about different theories, from learning theory to critical theory. We also go through peer observations of teaching and have in-depth discussion with our peers about what is happening in our classrooms and how we can improve.

Critical Information Literacy

Critical information literacy (CIL) incorporates critical pedagogies into the library classroom through approach, content, and assessment. While its basis is in critical theory, CIL's specific theoretical foundations are in their infancy.[19] While the lack of specificity in a definition makes it difficult to summarize CIL neatly, it encourages the scholarly conversation surrounding critical information literacy to evolve and grow and fosters discussions that question the what, why, and how of our information literacy classrooms. We like Accardi, Drabinski, and Kumbier's description of CIL as "a library instruction praxis that promotes critical engagement with information sources, considers students collaborators in knowledge production practices (and creators in their own right), recognizes the affective dimensions of research, and (in some cases) has liberatory aims."[20] CIL is not a set of teachable skills or a distinct classroom strategy. It is a pedagogical foundation that combines information and action. However, CIL can move beyond the classroom to permeate other

---

18. hooks, *Teaching to Transgress*, 130.

19. Downey, *Critical Information Literacy*, 41.

20. Maria T. Accardi, Emily Drabinski, and Alana Kumbier, *Critical Library Instruction: Theories and Methods* (Duluth, MN: Library Juice Press, 2010), 11-12.

aspects of librarianship, such as cataloging, reference interactions, and collection development.[21] "Critical information literacy is, as is information, what we know and also what we do."[22] So what is it that the practicing critical information literacy librarian does? According to James Elmborg, a critical information literacy librarian takes a critical approach to how we view our students, information, and ourselves.[23] He claims that it is more about relationships between people and information, stating "as radical as it might seem, the critical information literacy librarian may come to believe that we have no 'thing' to teach to students. The critical information librarian will instead participate in Freire's ongoing questioning and struggling for meaning."[24]

Embracing critical information literacy as a practical philosophy can be difficult. Academic librarians often confront unique scenarios that limit our ability to fully engage in critically-minded pedagogy. Time constraints and expectations of discipline-specific teaching faculty can disproportionately influence the pedagogical decisions of a critical information literacy librarian. As Elizabeth Peterson asked, "How can I both cover relevant material and engage in activities that encourage students to question the underlying political hegemony of the classroom/library/university/society – in 50 minutes?"[25]

---

21. Eamon Tewell, email message to author, June 2016.

22. Jessica Critten, "Introduction," In *Critical Information Literacy: Foundations, Inspiration, and Ideas*, by Annie Downey (Sacramento, CA: Library Juice Press, 2016), 6.

23. James Elmborg, "Critical Information Literacy: Definitions and Challenges," in *Transforming Information Literacy Programs: Intersecting Frontiers of Self, Library Culture, and Campus Community*, ed. Carroll Wetzel Wilkinson and Courtney Bruch (Chicago: Association of College and Research Libraries), 93-94.

24. Elmborg, "Critical Information Literacy," 94.

25. Elizabeth Peterson, "Problem-Based Learning as Teaching Strategy," in *Critical Library Instruction: Theories and Method*, eds. Maria T. Accardi, Emily Drabinski, and Alana Kumbier (Duluth, MN: Library Juice Press, 2010), 71-80.

Critical-Inclusive Pedagogical Framework

Dr. Saran Stewart developed the Critical-Inclusive Pedagogical Framework (CIPF)[26] (see **Figure 1**) based on the tenets of inclusive pedagogy outlined by Dr. Frank Tuitt, which include Faculty-Student Interaction, Sharing Power, Dialogical Professor-Student Interaction, Activation of Student Voice, and Utilization of Student Narrative.[27] Stewart designed the CIPF in order to "develop a conceptual and theoretical base in which to engage students in higher education as co-constructors in the teaching-learning process."[28] We've adapted her original representation of the CIPF to emphasize the holistic nature of the five tenets:

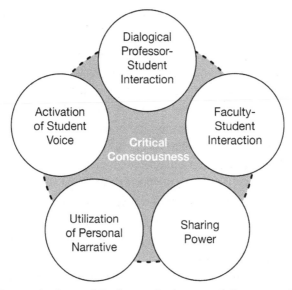

Figure 1: Critical-Inclusive Pedagogical Framework[29]

26. Dr. Stewart earned her Ph.D. from the University of Denver. She is currently lecturer of Comparative Higher Education in the School of Education at the University of the West Indies.

27. Frank Tuitt, "Afterword: Realizing a More Inclusive Pedagogy," in *Race and Higher Education: Rethinking Pedagogy in Diverse College Classrooms*, eds. Annie Howell and Frank Tuitt (Cambridge, MA: Harvard Education Publishing Group, 2003), 243-268.

28. Stewart, "Advancing a Critical and Inclusive Praxis," 11.

29. Stewart, "Advancing a Critical and Inclusive Praxis," 12.

The goal of the CIPF is what Freire called *conscientização*, or critical consciousness, "which encompasses being aware of power relations, analyzing habits of thinking, challenging discursive and ideological formations, and taking initiative."[30] The attainment of critical consciousness comes through engaged, dialogue-driven education that "problematizes generative themes from everyday life, topical issues from society, and academic subject matter from specific disciplines."[31] This critical pedagogy emphasizes student engagement and "stresses the importance of disagreeing, challenging ideas, and understanding the viewpoints of others to better confront societal issues."[32] While it may not be possible for students to achieve critical consciousness through information literacy one-shot instruction, or even through credit-bearing courses, it is something that we can foster through our pedagogical practice. Stewart stresses that critical consciousness is developed over time, not just in one course, stating that it "can resemble an oscillating pendulum, because in any given moment, one's critical consciousness can shift according to recognition of himself or herself in society amid revolving societal changes."[33] Similarly, Jodi Kaufmann advises patience, noting that because "critical consciousness is often invisible, hidden outside the purview of the instructor...one needs to have faith that critical seeds have been planted because one does not know when, where, and how critical consciousness will manifest."[34]

All tenets of the CIPF are strategies that teachers can incorporate individually in the classroom. However, Stewarts' Framework is significant in that it looks at the tenets holistically, as interconnected. Together the tenets of the CIPF serve as a

---

30. Jodi Jan Kaufmann, "The Practice of Dialogue in Critical Pedagogy," *Adult Education Quarterly: A Journal of Research and Theory* 60, no. 5 (2010): 458.

31. Kaufmann, "The Practice of Dialogue in Critical Pedagogy," 458.

32. Myra Dutko, "I Matter, As Does the World: Critical Consciousness in Higher Education" (PhD diss., National Louis University, 2016), 13, http://digitalcommons.nl.edu/diss/182.

33. Stewart, "Advancing a Critical and Inclusive Praxis," 13.

34. Kaufmann, "The Practice of Dialogue in Critical Pedagogy," 471.

guide for critical pedagogues and help us to create a pedagogy that works toward critical consciousness. What follows is an in-depth discussion of each tenet.

Activation of Student Voice

It is not always clear what people mean when they talk about student voice,[35] and there is minimal literature about student voice in higher education.[36] Giroux sees student voice as students "naming [their] own reality and talking about things that are important to their lives."[37] Focusing his work on public schooling, Giroux places the responsibility on teachers to learn about their school's community so that issues affecting students are discussed in the classroom. The teacher activates student voice by centering on discussions important to students. McLaren defines voice as "the cultural grammar and background knowledge that individuals use to interpret and articulate experience."[38] Jane Seale notes that voice entails "listening to and valuing the views that students express regarding their learning experiences; communicating student views to people who are in a position to influence change; and treating students as equal partners in the evaluation of teaching and learning, thus empowering them to take a more active role in shaping or changing their education."[39] Voice is the recognition that each student brings unique experiences and can contribute valuable perspectives on learning. Centering students' voice acknowledges "student point-of-view and experience, a strategy that stands in

35. Julie McLeod, "Student Voice and the Politics of Listening in Higher Education," *Critical Studies in Education* 52, no. 2 (2011): 179-189.

36. Jane Seale, "Doing Student Voice Work in Higher Education: An Exploration of the Value of Participatory Methods," *British Educational Research Journal* 36, no. 6 (December 2010): 995-1015.

37. Henry A. Giroux, "Teacher Education and Democratic Schooling," in *The Critical Pedagogy Reader*, eds. Antonia Darder, Marta P. Baltodano, and Rodolfo D. Torres (New York: Routledge, 2009), 454.

38. Peter McLaren, *Life in Schools*, 6th ed. (Boulder, CO: Paradigm Publishers, 2015), 180.

39. Seale, "Doing Student Voice Work in Higher Education," 995.

contrast to responding only to teacher or bureaucratically-driven conceptions of learning."[40]

Although we are not providing an in-depth discussion of them in this chapter, a number of educators have brought up concerns about student voice[41] and argue that more theorizing needs to be done around student voice work in higher education.[42] There is a concern about what counts as voice and which or whose voices are recognized.[43] There is also the concern that voice may be used as a means for control instead of for democratic inclusivity.[44] Julie McLeod is concerned that continuing to align conversations about voice with marginalized or underrepresented populations further stigmatizes these students.[45] Finally, teachers are concerned about doing harm to students by equating silence with voicelessness[46] and with silencing silence as a form of domination.[47] These critiques do not mean that activating student voice is something to avoid. Acknowledging that students have a voice and encouraging them to use it is essential to critical and inclusive pedagogies.[48] The key is to realize that it is not enough for students simply to talk. We must listen. Active listening is essential to dialogue and "being listened to" tells students that their voices matter and helps to motivate

---

40. McLeod, "Student Voice and the Politics of Listening in Higher Education," 186.

41. Elizabeth Ellsworth, "Why Doesn't This Feel Empowering? Working Through the Repressive Myths of Critical Pedagogy," *Harvard Educational Review* 59, no. 3 (1989): 297-325; Michael Fielding, "Transformative Approaches to Student Voice: Theoretical Underpinnings, Recalcitrant Realities," *British Educational Research Journal* 30, no. 2 (2004): 295-311; McLeod, "Student Voice and the Politics of Listening in Higher Education"; and Carol Robinson and Carol Taylor, "Theorizing Student Voice: Values and Perspectives," *Improving Schools* 10, no. 1 (2007): 5-17.

42. Fielding, "Transformative Approaches to Student Voice"; and Robinson and Taylor, "Theorizing Student Voice."

43. McLeod, "Student Voice and the Politics of Listening in Higher Education"; and Ellsworth, "Why Doesn't This Feel Empowering?"

44. Robinson and Taylor, "Theorizing Student Voice."

45. McLeod, "Student Voice and the Politics of Listening in Higher Education."

46. Ellsworth, "Why Doesn't This Feel Empowering?"

47. Kaufmann, "The Practice of Dialogue in Critical Pedagogy."

48. Tuitt, "Afterword: Realizing a More Inclusive Pedagogy."

participation.[49] Nick Couldry states, "one of the banal oxymorons of neoliberal democracy is the paradox that voice can apparently be offered, without any attention to whether it is matched by processes for listening to, and registering, voice."[50] As McLeod states, "if we want to court student voice we have to respond with something beyond a course evaluation questionnaire."[51] Engaging in dialogue with our students, or what Jennifer Bain calls "opportunity for voice,"[52] is how we encourage students to participate and contribute to the classroom.

Dialogical Professor-Student Interaction

Like Freire (and hooks, and Stewart, and Tuitt), we hope to deconstruct the traditional student/teacher relationship that is developed with the banking model of education.[53] Dialogical interaction is more than a conversation that two people have walking down the street.[54] It is also distinct from dialogue that reinforces a one-way discussion between two unequals. Dialogic interaction is about relationships between equals that promotes critique with the aim of creating collaborative learning environments.[55] We strive to center student voice in both learning and assessment and to create a classroom environment where students and teachers are partners

49. Ira Shor, *When Students Have Power: Negotiating Authority in Critical Pedagogy* (Chicago: The University of Chicago Press, 1996), 49.

50. Nick Couldry, "Rethinking the Politics of Voice," *Continuum: Journal of Media and Cultural Studies* 23, no. 4 (2009): 581.

51. McLeod, "Student Voice and the Politics of Listening in Higher Education," 187.

52. Jennifer Bain, "Integrating Student Voice: Assessment for Empowerment," *Practitioner Research in Higher Education* 4, no. 1 (2010): 18-19.

53.. Freire, *Pedagogy of the Oppressed*, 53.

54. Paulo Freire and Donaldo P. Macedo, "A Dialogue: Culture, Language, and Race," in *Breaking Free: The Transformative Power of Critical Pedagogy*, eds. Pepi Leistyna, Arlie Woodrum, and Stephen A. Sherblom (Cambridge, MA: Harvard Education Review, 1996), 199-228.

55. Catherine O'Connor and Sarah Michaels, "When is Dialogue 'Dialogic'?" *Human Development* 50 (2007): 275-285.; Saran Stewart, "Everything in Di Dark Muss Come to Light: A Postcolonial Investigation of the Practice of Extra Lessons at the Secondary Level in Jamaica's Education System." PhD Diss., University of Denver, 2013.

in learning and teaching.[56] Fostering partnerships with students and ensuring that we engage in dialogue with our students about the classroom and the curriculum "gives students an opportunity to engage in democratic practices as well as democratic ways of being."[57] Dialogical interaction is essential to creating a classroom where everyone can succeed; meaningful dialogue is what allows us to confront barriers and start to form a collaborative community in the classroom.[58] For Tuitt, "the dialogical process seeks to create respectful, challenging, and collaborative learning environments and to ensure that there is mutual professor-student participation."[59] Downey's recent work on critical information literacy highlights dialogue as one of the teaching approaches used by librarians to teach critical information literacy.[60] Librarians in Downey's study use dialogue to "help students form a meaningful connection with the material or to find ways that they may already be personally invested in the ideas and concepts being discussed." They also use dialogue to give students "a voice in their own learning experience."[61]

Faculty-Student Interaction

In the traditional college classroom, there is little teacher-student interaction because the class revolves around the activity and control of the professor.[62] Inversely, critical and inclusive pedagogues see students as partners in the learning process and work to share authority and power with students, as opposed

---

56. Alison Cook-Sather, Catherine Bovill, and Peter Felten, *Engaging Students as Partners in Learning and Teaching: A Guide for Faculty* (San Francisco: Josey-Bass, 2014).

57. Cook-Sather, Bovill, and Felten, *Engaging Students as Partners in Learning and Teaching*, 128.

58. hooks, *Teaching to Transgress*, 130.

59. Tuitt, "Afterword: Realizing a More Inclusive Pedagogy," 248.

60. Downey, *Critical Information Literacy*, 90.

61. Downey, *Critical Information Literacy*, 91.

62. Tuitt, Haynes, and Stewart, *Race, Equity and the Learning Environment*.

to demonstrating authority over them.[63] Building partnerships with students is a shift in our thinking from preparing them to be democratic citizens to realizing that they already are citizens, and that we need to engage with them as such.[64] Faculty-student interaction "promotes positive relationships between student and faculty."[65]

Sharing Power

Sharing power in the classroom does not come naturally. University structures impose a model of authority, and students who have been living in the system are not always prepared for the responsibility of shared power in the classroom.[66] Students may actively refuse to participate in this type of classroom and may see the professor as less effective, which causes some professors to stop trying.[67] Downey discusses librarians' experience with student resistance and how students "push back" when librarians try to implement a critical pedagogy.[68] We have certainly met resistance in our work. In a one-shot instruction session last year, Rachel began her class by asking the graduate students what they wanted from the session and a student replied, "you tell us, you're the teacher." Of course, we have also received positive feedback from students who find it refreshing to have a say in the course curriculum and assessment. In reflecting on collaboration in a credit course, one

---

63. Nancy Schniedewind, "Teaching Feminist Process," *Women's Studies Quarterly* 15, no. 3/4 (1987): 15-31.

64. Alison Hicks and Caroline Sinkinson, "Reflections on the Retention Narrative: Extending Critical Pedagogy beyond the Classroom." In *Critical Library Pedagogy Handbook*, Volume 1, eds. Nicole Pagowsky and Kelly McElroy (Chicago: Association of College and Research Libraries, 2016), 171-183.

65. Stewart, "Advancing a Critical and Inclusive Praxis," 14.

66. Stewart, "Advancing a Critical and Inclusive Praxis," 15.

67. hooks, *Teaching to Transgress,* 187-188.

68. Downey, *Critical Information Literacy,* 103.

of Lyda's students commented that "being included in the course design as a student is essential in making a good class."[69]

We've struggled with how to share power with students without also giving up our own agency. We appreciate the work of Alison Cook-Sather, Catherine Bovill, and Peter Felten who have written extensively on creating partnerships with students. Through their work, we understand more fully how we can share power with students by partnering with them in the process of teaching and learning. Partnerships require respect, reciprocity, and shared responsibility, all of which goes both ways.[70] This notion is also seen in the work of hooks, who believes that sharing power is about students recognizing their responsibility for their own learning and making the classroom a democratic space where everyone feels a responsibility to contribute.[71] We've come to see that we must acknowledge our roles as experts, as well as the power we have as faculty. To do otherwise, or to pretend a false equivalency, is to come into the classroom dishonestly. Discussing this in her own work, Stewart claims that "as the lecturer, I am also the oppressor with the assumed sole power to construct knowledge in the class. I control the direction of my students' learning and can either encourage or diminish inclusion."[72] Partnership, according to Cook-Sather, Bovill, and Felten, "does not require a false equivalency, but it does mean that the perspective and contributions made by partners are equally valued and respected."[73] We also must acknowledge the expertise of students, who are experts at being students, and whose experiences can expand our own understanding of teaching, learning, and assessment. To build effective partnerships with

---

69. Rachel Dineen and Lyda McCartin, "An Unfinished Journey: Becoming Critical Educators," in *Credit-Bearing Information Literacy Courses: Critical Approaches*, eds. Jessica Critten and Angela Pashia (ACRL, forthcoming, 2018).

70. Cook-Sather, Bovill, and Felten, *Engaging Students as Partners in Learning and Teaching*, 3.

71. hooks, *Teaching to Transgress*, 187-188.

72. Stewart, "Advancing a Critical and Inclusive Praxis," 12.

73. Cook-Sather, Bovill, and Felten, *Engaging Students as Partners in Learning and Teaching*, 7.

students we must "listen to students but also articulate our own expertise, perspectives, and commitments."[74]

Utilization of Student Narrative

Student voice and student narrative are similar in that both seek to centralize student experience. Narrative is different from voice in that it is about personal reflection that leads to making connections between personal experience and new information gained in the classroom. The crux of this tenet is that "one's own experience is central to understanding and developing knowledge."[75] Eamon Tewell illustrates the utilization of student narrative in his description of a class activity on examining bias in subject headings:[76]

> One class was researching the communities in Brooklyn and New York City that they've grown up in or currently live in, and how these communities have changed (or not) in terms of demographics. One of the resources they were using was NY Times Historical Newspapers, and so I did a search for a largely African-American neighborhood and noted the different subject headings that were ascribed to an article about the neighborhood, all negative and judgmental of the community's condition. I compared this search to one for an affluent White neighborhood and pointed out how differently the subject headings portrayed this area, and asked what that signals to people researching different areas of the city. Later while students were searching for information on their communities, one student pointed out how her neighborhood was depicted in a Times article as dirty, deteriorating, and crime-ridden. She grew up in and loved her neighborhood, and challenged this representation—she decided she was changing her paper topic from how the neighborhood had changed over the years into one

74. Cook-Sather, Bovill, and Felten, *Engaging Students as Partners in Learning and Teaching*, 9.

75. Mary Ann Danowitz and Frank Tuitt, "Enacting Inclusivity through Engaged Pedagogy: A Higher Education Perspective," *Equity & Excellence in Education* 44, no. 1 (2011): 49.

76. Eamon Tewell, email correspondence to author, June 21, 2016. This is also discussed by Tewell in a recent LOEX conference presentation. See Eamon Tewell, "The Problem with Grit: Dismantling Deficit Models in Information Literacy Instruction," (LOEX, Houston, TX, May 5, 2018).

about all of the good things in her community, like her church, social support services, community events, and the people that tie her community together. This was an important moment because the student recognized the racial bias inherent in a prominent, respected publication and chose to refute that representation by providing counter-evidence.

Stewart describes student narrative as teachers knowing about the lives of students outside of the classroom and using that knowledge to enhance course content. Using student experience leads to increased student engagement and better relationships between students and teachers.[77]

Wrap-Up

In this chapter we discussed the mindset of critical practice, which includes a dedication to reflexive and flexible teaching, reflection, and dialogue. While we've referred to authors who may be familiar to librarians, such as Freire, hooks, and Shor, we hope the introduction of other critical pedagogues, specifically Stewart and Tuitt, opens up a new realm of literature for critical librarians. The Critical-Inclusive Pedagogical Framework (CIPF) is the foundation of our teaching and assessment practice. You'll notice that in our discussion of the CIPF we provided more in-depth discussions about the tenets Sharing Power and Activation of Student Voice. These two tenets are, for us, the most important of the five because they are central to breaking down the traditional relationship between student and teacher—without them, achievement of the other tenets may not be possible. These two tenets are also where we've struggled the most in our practice, because up to this point we've been rooted in the traditional hegemonic power structures of higher education and breaking from this requires that we reflect on our identities, privileges, and role in the classroom. You will see our work mapped to the five tenets of the CIPF throughout the book.

---

77. Stewart, "Everything in Di Dark Muss Come to Light," 245.

Chapter 2

ASSESSMENT OF TEACHING AND LEARNING

Essentially, assessment is the "systematic collection, review, and use of information about educational programs undertaken for the purpose of improving learning and development."[1] For us, assessment is so much more. It is "a framework for focusing faculty attention on student learning and for provoking meaningful discussion of program objectives, curricular organization, pedagogy, and student development."[2] For us, assessment is a dialogic collaboration between faculty and students "that builds consensus and shapes a sense of purpose"[3] and a process that ignites "intellectual curiosity about what and how well our students learn."[4] Assessment is about improving learning, but it is also about improving teaching. A commitment to assessing student learning can lead to meaningful changes as an instructor. As Megan Oakleaf writes: "the practice of focusing on student learning goals and outcomes, assessing student attainment of learning outcomes, and

1. Catherine A. Palomba and Trudy W. Banta, *Assessment Essentials: Planning, Implementing, and Improving Assessment in Higher Education* (San Francisco: Jossey-Bass Publishers, 1999), 1.

2. Mary J. Allen, *Assessing Academic Programs in Higher Education* (Bolton, MA: Anker Publishing, 2004), 4.

3. Hardin L. Aasand, Stevens Amidon, and Debra Huffman, "Slouching Toward Assessment: One Department's Journey Toward Accountability Bliss," in *Coming to Terms with Student Outcomes Assessment: Faculty and Administrators' Journeys to Integrating Assessment in their Work and Institutional Culture*, ed. Peggy L. Maki (Sterling, VA: Stylus Publishing, 2010), 109.

4. Peggy L. Maki, *Assessing for Learning: Building a Sustainable Commitment Across the Institution* (Sterling, VA: Stylus Publishing, 2004), 2.

implementing instructional changes to increase student learning leads to the ongoing improvement of teaching skills."[5] Assessment of student learning is a necessary part of education and is vital to educational practice. It is also "the most political of all educational processes; it is where issues of power are most at stake."[6] The traditional model of assessment in higher education is a form of unilateral control that can be seen as a form of exploitation or oppression.[7] Thus, "the discourse of critical pedagogy is little more than empty rhetoric without serious attention to assessment practices."[8]

Unfortunately, most of the literature on critical information literacy offers little practical advice about assessing student learning critically. There are a few exceptions, however. Accardi outlines how a feminist approach can be applied to traditional classroom assessment techniques to allow students more opportunities for self-assessment and reflection.[9] She also discusses assessment methods that allow students to demonstrate their learning journeys in their own words.[10] We found it particularly encouraging to read in the *Critical Library Pedagogy Handbook*[11] that each lesson plan included a section on assessment. In reading these sections, however, many authors simply discussed how their critically-focused lesson could be assessed but did not discuss an actual critical approach they took

5. Megan Oakleaf, "The Information Literacy Instruction Assessment Cycle: A Guide for Increasing Student Learning and Improving Librarian Instructional Skills," *Journal of Documentation* 65, no. 4 (2009): 541.

6. John Heron, "Assessment," Working Paper (1979), quoted in Michael Reynolds and Kiran Trehan, "Assessment: A Critical Perspective," *Studies in Higher Education* 25, no. 3 (2000): 268.

7. John Heron, "Assessment Revisited" in *Developing Student Autonomy in Learning*, ed. David Boud (London: Kogan Page, 1988), 77-90.

8. Eloísa Lorente-Catalán and David Kirk, "Making the Case for Democratic Assessment Practices within a Critical Pedagogy of Physical Education Teacher Education," *European Physical Education Review* 20, no. 1 (2014): 114.

9. Accardi, *Feminist Pedagogy for Library Instruction*, 84-87.

10. Accardi, *Feminist Pedagogy for Library Instruction*, 84-87.

11. Nicole Pagowsky and Kelly McElroy, ed., *Critical Library Pedagogy Handbook*.

to the assessment.[12] In many lesson plans, the authors do not discuss their assessment process. Few go beyond formative observations, and do not provide a discussion of how they did the observations or how they use this data. Even when authors mention assessing sessions by getting feedback from faculty, there is no discussion of how this is done, and no examples of surveys are in the appendices. Student reflection in these lesson plans seem relegated to the basic minute-paper questions that include *what did you learn in this session?* Zoe Fisher describes this as a "service-oriented question." This information can be helpful, but it is important for students to reflect more deeply on their learning. Fisher recommends that librarians move to "learning-oriented questions" that go beyond satisfaction and confidence.[13] Examples of learning-oriented questions include: *What will you do differently, based on what you learned today? What are the next three steps you'll take with your project/assignment after today's session?*[14]

We know that, "although critical educators do not want to be bound by neoliberal assessment measures, they do want to determine how well they and their students are meeting critical course goals."[15] What appears to have happened in critical pedagogy is that there has been change in content and teaching methods, but far less change in assessment practice.[16] Thus, it is essential that we

---

12. Notable deviations from this trend can be seen in the following chapters of Pagowsky and McElroy, *Critical Library Pedagogy Handbook*: Lauren Wallis (Chapter 1), Eamon Tewell and Katelyn Angell (Chapter 7), Gina Schlesselman Tarango and Frances Suderman (Chapter 8), Christine Photinos (Chapter 9), Jacob Berg (Chapter 11), Dory Cochran (Chapter 14), Xan Goodman (Chapter 17), Ilana Stonebraker, Caitlán Maxwell, and Jessica Jerrit (Chapter 18), Erin Pappas, Celia Emmelhainz, and Maura Seale (Chapter 23), Angela Pashia (Chapter 24), Lydia Willoughby and Kelly Blanchat (Chapter 26), and Rachel Gammons (Chapter 30).

13. Zoe Fisher, "Learning is Not a Service" (Library Assessments and Metrics Workshop, Colorado Academic Library Association, Denver, CO, November 18, 2016). https://quickaskzoe.com/speaking/.

14. Fisher, "Learning is Not a Service," slide 16.

15. D. H. Kahl Jr., "Critical Communication Pedagogy and Assessment: Reconciling Two Seemingly Incongruous Ideas," *International Journal of Communication* 7, no. 1 (2013): 2615.

16. Reynolds and Trehan, "Assessment a Critical Perspective," 268.

explore alternative assessment methods that align with our critical perspective, and that we are constantly practicing self-reflection and inviting our peers to observe and critique our teaching. Assessment "should be frequent and rigorous"[17] but focused on student-centered methods instead of standardized tests. In this chapter we discuss approaches to critical assessment through a review of the literature on methods for assessing teaching and methods for assessing student learning through a critical lens.[18]

Approaches to Critical Assessment

Eloisa Lorente-Catalan and David Kirk note: "to achieve democratic and educative assessment in the classroom means to create a community of shared practice where nothing of the assessment process is hidden from the students and they can assess their own learning."[19] Linda Keesing-Styles outlines multiple themes that are essential components to critical assessment:[20]

1. Focuses on dialogue between students and teachers
2. Shares roles and responsibilities of the classroom between teachers and students, ensuring all voices are heard
3. Combines theory and practice in classroom assessment

17. Ira Shor, *Empowering Education: Critical Teaching for Social Change* (Chicago: University of Chicago Press, 1992): 144.

18. For a discussion of traditional assessment practice in information literacy see Oakleaf, "The Information Literacy Instruction Assessment Cycle"; a more recent literature review on assessment practice in the information literacy classroom is Allison Erlinger, "Outcomes Assessment in Undergraduate Information Literacy Instruction: A Systematic Review," *College & Research Libraries* 79, no. 4 (2018): 442-479.

19. Lorente-Catalán and Kirk, "Making the Case for Democratic Assessment Practices," 108.

20. Linda Keesing-Styles, "The Relationship Between Critical Pedagogy and Assessment in Teacher Education," *Radical Pedagogy* 5, no. 1 (2003): 10. These concepts are seen in the list compiled by Carolyn Caffrey Gardner and Rebecca Halpern outlining the values and practices that assessment should follow as a part of a critical praxis. One notable difference is the inclusion of a reflective component in Gardner and Halpern. We agree that reflection is an essential feature of critical assessment methods. Carolyn Caffrey Gardner and Rebecca Halpern, "At Odds with Assessment: Being a Critical Educator within the Academy," in *Critical Library Pedagogy Handbook*, Volume 1, eds. Nicole Pagowsky and Kelly McElroy, 41-51.

4. Acknowledges, validates, and centers student experience
5. Is problem-posing, linking hegemonic institutional structures and systematic oppression
6. Examines and reinterprets power dynamics
7. Values negotiation of curriculum and assessment so that students and teachers feel as though they have been a part of the process

This type of approach to assessment is not easy. We must not only be partners with our students, but we must allow our students to adapt to this type of alternative assessment in their own way. We must anticipate some pushback from those students who may be accustomed to traditional assessment practices. We must also be cognizant of how our methods affect our students and shape our mindsets. This reflection helps to ensure that we are working toward empowering both our students and ourselves.

Assessment of Teaching

In their seminal work on classroom assessment, Thomas Angelo and Patricia Cross state: "the quality of student learning is directly, although not exclusively, related to the quality of teaching. Therefore, one of the most promising ways to improve learning is to improve teaching."[21] They further state that teachers need to seek "specific, comprehensible feedback" on their practice.[22] While we can learn much about our teaching from student learning assessment, it is essential to effective practice that we assess our teaching. Just like with learning assessment, teaching assessment can be formative or summative. Summative assessment is focused more on evaluation of teaching and is not necessarily useful for improving practice. Formative assessment of teaching is most helpful for improving practice because we are working on our own growth and development, and focusing on our own concerns

---

21. Thomas A. Angelo and K. Patricia Cross, *Classroom Assessment Techniques*, 2nd ed. (San Francisco: Jossey-Bass, 1993), 7.

22. Angelo and Cross, *Classroom Assessment Techniques*, 8.

about teaching. For the formative assessment of our teaching, we rely on reflection and peer observation. These methods require an open mind, a willingness to accept critical feedback, and a desire to change practice.

Reflection

The practice of reflection is "deliberate and intentional" thinking.[23] It is a "deliberate pause" needed for "higher-level thinking."[24] Reflection is used to interpret, analyze, and question the way we work because without reflection, our teaching remains unexamined.[25] One of the best pieces we've read about reflection is Michelle Reale's work on becoming a reflective teacher and librarian.[26] Reale makes reflective practice approachable by bringing together seminal works and adding personal stories of her own journey in reflective practice. Reale notes that reflection is dialogic, a dialogue with others and ourselves.[27] She encourages dialogue through journaling. We have chosen journaling as our go-to method of reflection, because it provides us with a record of our thinking over time. What we have written is stored away and can be read, reread, and shared.[28] We've realized that the best reflection is done together; we get more out of our reflections when we talk out our questions with each other. Ultimately, this leads us to a better solution. While the most common method of reflection

23. Michelle Reale, *Becoming a Reflective Librarian and Teacher: Strategies for Mindful Academic Practice* (Chicago: ALA Editions, 2017), 2.

24. York-Barr et al., *Reflective Practice to Improve Schools*, 6.

25. Reale, *Becoming a Reflective Librarian and Teacher*, 2.

26. Reale, *Becoming a Reflective Librarian and Teacher*.

27. Reale, *Becoming a Reflective Librarian and Teacher*, 82.

28. Margaret E.S. Forrest, "Learning and Teaching in Action: On Becoming a Critically Reflective Teacher," *Health Information and Libraries Journal* 25, no. 3 (2008): 229-232.

is personal journaling,[29] there is also discussion in the literature on video recording for reflective practice,[30] as well as poetry, narrative, and drawing.[31] Regardless of how you choose to engage in reflective practice, it seems evident from the literature that reflection improves practice by helping us to understand ourselves, which helps us to better manage and support change.[32]

Reflection is not just about improving teaching methods, it is also essential to understanding ourselves as teachers. Journaling lets teachers reflect on what shapes our pedagogical philosophies as well as what values and assumptions we bring into the classroom or are imposing on our students. Critical pedagogues must continuously reflect on their power and positionality in order to maintain a critical mindset in the classroom.[33] This is neither an easy nor a cursory task. Reflection requires dedicated time and a commitment to questioning the roles we undertake as teachers. It "involves the conscious consideration of the moral and ethical implications and consequences of classroom practices on students."[34]

29. Elizabeth K. Tompkins, "A Reflective Teaching Journal: An Instructional Improvement Tool for Academic Librarians," *College & Undergraduate Libraries* 16, no. 4 (2009): 221-238; Reale, *Becoming a Reflective Librarian and Teacher*; Accardi and Reale, "Critical Reflection to Improve and Grow as Librarians Who Teach"; Mandi Goodsett, "Reflective Teaching: Improving Library Instruction Through Self-Reflection," *Southeastern Librarian* 62, no. 3 (2014): 12-15; and Forrest, "Learning and Teaching in Action."

30. Goodsett, "Reflective Teaching"; Cheryl L. Rosaen et al., "Noticing Noticing: How Does Investigation of Video Records Change How Teachers Reflect on Their Experiences?," *Journal of Teacher Education* 59, no. 4 (2008): 347-360; and John F. McCullagh, "How Can Video Supported Reflection Enhance Teachers' Professional Development?," *Cultural Studies of Science Education* 7, no. 1 (2012): 137-152.

31. Reale, *Becoming a Reflective Librarian and Teacher*, 60-1; Accardi and Reale, "Critical Reflection to Improve and Grow as Librarians Who Teach," webinar presented for ALA Connect, June 2, 2017.

32. Maria J. Grant, "The Role of Reflection in the Library and Information Sector: A Systematic Review," *Health Information & Libraries Journal* 24, no. 3 (2007): 155-166; Anne Jumonville Graf and Benjamin Harris, "Reflective Assessment: Opportunities and Challenges," *Reference Services Review* 44, no. 1 (2016): 38-47; and Tompkins, "A Reflective Teaching Journal."

33. Kyoko Kishimoto, "Anti-Racist Pedagogy: From Faculty's Self-Reflection to Organizing within and Beyond the Classroom," *Race Ethnicity and Education* 21, no. 4 (2018): 540.

34. Barbara Larrivee, "Transforming Teaching Practice: Becoming the Critically Reflective Teacher," *Reflective Practice* 1, no. 3 (2000): 294.

Reflection can be uncomfortable. Examining deeply held beliefs is hard, and changing attitudes and behaviors takes time. Whenever we question our work or think about a difficult conversation we just had, we remember Barbara Larivee's advice that "in order to break through familiar cycles, one has to allow oneself to feel confused and anxious—not permanently, but for a time. Fully experiencing this sense of uncertainty is what opens the door to a personal deeper understanding, leading to a shift in ways of thinking and perceiving."[35] We know that reflection can be difficult and that it can also lead to more work, but we also know that reflection is rewarding. It has forced us to have serious conversations about our privilege and our identities in the classroom and has improved our practice. For us, reflection has instilled a professional trust in each other that we would not have had otherwise.

Peer Observation of Teaching

Before we began assessing our teaching, we focused more energy on the act of teaching than learning about our teaching. However, learning from others, particularly our peers and our students, transforms our pedagogy. A familiar technique for engaging in this type of learning is peer observation. There are many names for peer observation and a number of ways to approach the process. Some call it peer observation,[36] while others deem it peer coaching,[37] and

---

35. Larivee, "Transforming Teaching Practice," 304.

36. Sue Samson and Donna E. McCrea, "Using Peer Review to Foster Good Teaching," *Reference Services Review* 36, no. 1 (2008): 61-70; Jaena Alabi and William H. Weare Jr., "Peer Review of Teaching: Best Practices for a Non-Programmatic Approach," *Communications in Information Literacy* 8, no. 2 (2014): 180-191; and Linda Norbury, "Peer Observation of Teaching: A Method for Improving Teaching Quality," *New Review of Academic Librarianship* 7, no. 1 (2001): 87-99.

37.Caroline Sinkinson, "An Assessment of Peer Coaching to Drive Professional Development and Reflective Teaching," *Communications in Information Literacy* 5, no. 1 (2011): 9-20; Dale J. Vidmar, "Reflective Peer Coaching: Crafting Collaborative Self-Assessment in Teaching," *Research Strategies* 20, no. 3 (2006): 135-148; and Priscilla Finley et al., "Enhancing library instruction with Peer planning," *Reference Services Review* 33, no. 1 (2005): 112-122.

others use a Critical Friends Group model.[38] By peer observation, we mean the practice of watching a colleague in the classroom with the expressed goal of teaching improvement. We are not referring to any observation used for summative assessment or any supervisory observation used to make staffing decisions. While we accept that evaluation happens for these reasons, we approach peer observation with two purposes—to build a trusting relationship with colleagues and to improve our own practice.

Regardless of what we call it or how we do it, it is clear from the literature that this method of formative teaching assessment has many benefits. In their discussion of a Peer Review of Teaching (PROT) program, Sue Samson and Donna McCrea indicate that the program inspired their faculty, encouraged mentoring, and fostered a commitment to improvement.[39] They also note that participants in the program mentioned being more self-critical of their teaching, indicating that peer observation could lead to increased self-reflection. These themes are seen throughout the literature.[40] Caroline Sinkinson discusses a program at the University of Colorado (CU) Boulder designed specifically to increase reflection and foster a community of teachers intent on improving practice. This program was also developed to reduce the sense of isolation experienced by librarians who teach.[41] In fact, peer coaching has been discussed in the library literature since the 1980s, both in relation to reference service and teaching, especially to prevent classroom isolation for those librarians who found

---

38. Yvonne Hultman Özek, Gudrun Edgren, and Katarina Jandér, "Implementing the Critical Friend Method for Peer Feedback among Teaching Librarians in an Academic Setting," *Evidence Based Library and Information Practice* 7, no. 4 (2012): 68-81.

39. Samson and McCrea, "Using Peer Review to Foster Good Teaching."

40. Samson and McCrea, "Using Peer Review to Foster Good Teaching"; Sinkinson, "An Assessment of Peer Coaching to Drive Professional Development and Reflective Teaching"; Lee-Allison Levene and Polly Frank, "Peer Coaching: Professional Growth and Development for Instruction Librarians," *Reference Services Review* 21, no. 3 (1993): 35-42; Norbury, "Peer Observation of Teaching"; Vidmar, "Reflective Peer Coaching"; and Deborah Bambino, "Critical Friends," *Educational Leadership* 59, no. 6 (2002): 25-27.

41. Sinkinson, "An Assessment of Peer Coaching to Drive Professional Development and Reflective Teaching," 10.

themselves in the teaching role.[42] Peer observation continues to be helpful in addressing the issue of librarians having little formal teacher training.[43]

Most of these peer observation programs follow Graham Martin and Jeremy Doubles' model of holding a pre-meeting, observation, then holding a post-meeting.[44] However, we do see modifications on this model in the library literature. Dale Vidmar promotes a reflective peer-coaching model.[45] In this model, there is no observation. Instead, two librarians engage in dialogue during a planning conversation and a post-teaching reflective conference in order to "examine intentions prior to teaching and reflection afterward."[46] In the planning conversation before the session, the teacher shares their intentions and goals. The lesson plan takes shape through conversation about teaching methods and approach. After the teaching session, there is a reflective conference where the instructor reflects on what happened in order to determine if their goals were met.

Peer coaching may be a good model to implement if you are working with librarians who are intimidated by being observed or are hesitant to participate in a peer observation process. Intimidation is a real concern and should be considered when putting together a peer feedback program.[47] This model will also promote self-reflection and self-assessment in librarians. Combining these two models may alleviate the stress associated with peer observation, since there is more trust built between teacher and coach before the observation. The CU Boulder pilot indicates that librarians who participated felt more self-reflective because of the program, with

42. Finley et al., "Enhancing Library Instruction with Peer Planning."

43. Alabi and Weare, "Peer Review of Teaching."

44. Graham A. Martin and Jeremy M. Double, "Developing Higher Education Teaching Skills through Peer Observation and Collaborative Reflection," *Innovations in Education & Training International* 35, no. 2 (1998): 161-170.

45. Vidmar, "Reflective Peer Coaching."

46. Vidmar, "Reflective Peer Coaching," 146.

47. Sinkinson, "An Assessment of Peer Coaching to Drive Professional Development and Reflective Teaching," 17.

one librarian noting, "I'm discovering now that I'm still thinking about my teaching, several weeks after teaching finished for the semester....I discovered that I can think of changes on my own and that I can maybe make differences in the future."[48]

Another model of peer observation is the Critical Friend model. A critical friend is a "trusted person who asks provocative questions, provides data to be examined through another lens, and offers critique of a person's work as a friend."[49] Critical Friends Groups grew in popularity among primary and secondary teachers as a way to get feedback about teaching by reflecting on the work of both teachers and students.[50] Supporters of the Critical Friends model indicate that these groups "establish a reflective community" and "create opportunities for colleagues to challenge their own practice."[51] In her discussion of a Critical Friends Group at C.W. Henry Elementary School in Philadelphia, Deborah Bambino noted that her experience with more self-reflection and critical conversations led her to more critical pedagogical methods such as designing rubrics and assignments with her students.[52] Librarians at Lund University in Sweden implemented a Critical Friend model with peer observation in response to the shift in the profession to more teaching by librarians.[53] For these librarians, self-reflection and self-assessment is important, but they like the Critical Friend model because it combines these practices with observation so that assessment is not done in isolation. It is clear from the literature on peer feedback models that, through this process, librarians improve their practice, become more confident in their teacher identity, and learn to be reflective about what they are doing in the classroom.

---

48. Sinkinson, "An Assessment of Peer Coaching to Drive Professional Development and Reflective Teaching," 8.

49. Arthur L. Costa and Bena Kallick, "Through the Lens of a Critical Friend," *Educational Leadership* 51, no. 2 (1993): 50.

50. Bambino, "Critical Friends."

51. Bambino, "Critical Friends," 27.

52. Bambino, "Critical Friends," 25-6.

53. Özek, Edgren, and Jandér, "Implementing the Critical Friend Method for Peer Feedback among Teaching Librarians in an Academic Setting," 69.

Peer feedback isn't the only feedback we should consider when it comes to improving our teaching. It is also important to get feedback from students, and it can be helpful to seek feedback from disciplinary faculty as well.[54] Research on peer observation indicates that when student feedback was viewed alongside peer feedback, it was easier to see the student feedback more constructively.[55] This may be because participation in peer observation leads to more self-reflection, which allows us to reflect more critically on what students say. We believe that eliciting feedback from those directly impacted by our teaching is essential, and we expand on this in the next chapter.

Assessment of Student Learning

Educators have long argued that traditional assessment methods were too authoritarian and reinforced social control from academic elites.[56] The 1980s and 1990s saw growth in literature on participative methods of assessment, which are generally self-, peer-, and co-assessment practices.[57] David Boud has written the seminal works on participative assessment, advocating for peer and self-assessment in higher education since the 1980s.[58] Boud sees self-assessment as "as much a learning activity as an assessment activity" and believes teachers should provide many opportunities for students to engage in self-assessment because it requires them "to think critically about what they are learning, to identify

---

54. Loanne Snavely and Nancy Dewald, "Developing and Implementing Peer Review of Academic Librarians' Teaching: An Overview and Case Report," *Journal of Academic Librarianship* 37, no. 4 (2011): 343-351.

55. Sullivan et al., "Peer Observation of Teaching as a Faculty Development Tool," *BMC Medical Education* 12, no. 1 (2012): 26.

56. Reynolds and Trehan, "Assessment," 267.

57. Reynolds and Trehan, "Assessment"; and Kelvin H. K. Tan, "Does Student Self-Assessment Empower Or Discipline Students?," *Assessment & Evaluation in Higher Education* 29, no. 6 (2004): 651-662.

58. David Boud, "The Role of Self-Assessment in Student Grading," *Studies in Higher Education* 14, no. 1 (1989): 20-30; David Boud, "Assessment and the Promotion of Academic Values," *Studies in Higher Education* 15, no. 1 (1990): 101-111; and David Boud, Ruth Cohen, and Jane Sampson, "Peer Learning and Assessment," *Assessment & Evaluation in Higher Education* 24, no. 4 (1999): 413-426.

appropriate standards of performance and to apply them to their own work."[59] He lauds self-assessment because it removes the teacher as the primary assessor in the classroom and lets students get involved in assessing their own performance. He believes this is important to achieving the goals of higher education, which include students developing the ability to evaluate their own work critically.[60] But, as Boud states, "we tend to believe that students do not have the capacity to assess their own learning, and that belief hinders their ability to ever do so."[61] It is important to note that self-assessment is not about the student assessing themselves in isolation; self-assessment is most effective when it involves peer assessment as well as assessment by an instructor.

Critical educators continue to explore participative assessment methods in higher education today.[62] Christine Brew and Philip Riley argue that participative assessment improves pedagogy "by encouraging reevaluation of the relationship between learning and assessment."[63] They contend that we should recognize the dual role assessment plays through formative and summative evaluations and work to reconstruct assessment, not as a method for students to reproduce memorized facts, but as a "demonstration of problem-solving, communication and presentation of skills."[64]

---

59. David Boud, *Implementing Student Self-Assessment* (Cambelltown, N.S.W.: Higher Education & Development Society of Australasia, 1991), 1.

60. Boud, Implementing Student Self-Assessment, 5.

61. Boud, "Assessment and the Promotion of Academic Values," 110.

62. Reynolds and Trehan, "Assessment"; Lorente-Catalán and Kirk, "Making the Case for Democratic Assessment Practices within a Critical Pedagogy of Physical Education Teacher Education"; Tan, "Does Student Self-Assessment Empower Or Discipline Students?"; Christine Brew and Philip Riley, "Measuring Student Support for Participative Assessment and Related Strategies: Development and Testing of the Beliefs About Participative Assessment Instrument (BAPAI)," *Australian Journal of Teacher Education* 36, no. 4 (2011): 33-52; and Keesing-Styles, "The Relationship Between Critical Pedagogy and Assessment in Teacher Education."

63. Brew and Riley, "Measuring Student Support for Participative Assessment and Related Strategies," 34.

64. Brew and Riley, "Measuring Student Support for Participative Assessment and Related Strategies," 34.

While research indicates that participative assessment methods are valuable,[65] these methods are not without critics. In their article about peer assessment, Michael Reynolds and Kirin Trehan advocate for participative assessment but note three concerns: (1) freedom may cause frustration and anxiety for students, (2) the teacher role must be carefully considered, and (3) inherent social processes and student-to-student power dynamics will exist and must be navigated.[66] Kelvin Tan critiques educators' assumptions that student participation in the assessment process enhances student empowerment.[67] Tan argues that learning rather than empowerment should be the focus of self-assessment, stating, "autonomy in student self-assessment should be viewed as a means to an end and not a goal in itself."[68] In a 2005 exploration of student stress and participative assessment methods, Nigel Pope found that peer- and self-assessment did induce stress for students. Pope's research also indicates that female students were more stressed than male students were when it came to self-assessment. However, Pope also found that students who undertook self-assessment had better summative assessment outcomes than students who did not go through self-assessment.[69] Despite the criticism, research on participative assessment suggests that "the advantages of participative assessment outweigh the shortcomings and concerns."[70] That said, it is important to consider the purpose of any assessment method as well as to consider student perceptions

---

65. Filip Dochy, M. Segers, and D. Sluijsmans, "The Use of Self-, Peer and Co-Assessment in Higher Education: A Review," *Studies in Higher Education* 21, no. 3 (1999): 331-350; Nancy Falchikov and Judy Goldfinch, "Student Peer Assessment in Higher Education: A Meta-Analysis Comparing Peer and Teacher Marks," *Review of Educational Research* 70, no. 3 (2000): 287-322; and Duncan D. Nulty, "Peer and Self-Assessment in the First Year of University," *Assessment & Evaluation in Higher Education* 36, no. 5 (2011): 493-507.

66. Reynolds and Trehan, "Assessment," 272-273.

67. Tan, "Does Student Self-assessment Empower Or Discipline Students?," 651.

68. Tan, "Does Student Self-assessment Empower Or Discipline Students?," 660.

69. Nigel K. Ll. Pope, "The Impact of Stress in Self- and Peer Assessment," *Assessment & Evaluation in Higher Education* 30, no. 1 (2005): 51-63.

70. Brew and Riley, "Measuring Student Support for Participative Assessment and Related Strategies," 34.

of methods. Brew and Riley's work measuring student support for participative methods reveals "modest support for the practice."[71] They recommend entering into a dialogue with students about support for these methods before implementing them in a course, which is a recommendation that is in line with critical practice. Participative assessment methods are not the only alternative assessment methods critical educators are exploring. Keesing-Styles presents examples of critical assessment from her own practice. She advocates student involvement in assessment through student-generated assessment criteria, in which students determine knowledge, skills, and dispositions for learning as well as through student-generated assessment tasks during which students decide how they will demonstrate their own learning. She also supports removing student learning outcomes from courses because, as a style of assessment, "it dictates what students learn and how they learn it, it focuses students' attention on assessment rather than learning, and it creates a degree of conformity."[72] In removing learning outcomes and focusing on the overall aims of the course, students can take more ownership over their own learning. It is important to note that Keesing-Styles is discussing assessment practice that is integrated into a teacher education degree program, and some of these methods may not work outside of a degree-granting program.

In a discussion about critical assessment that applies Freire's concept of *conscientização* to assessment procedures, David Kahl discusses the use of reflective journals, dialogue, and auto-ethnographic writing for assessment as possible methods to assess critical outcomes, such as heightened awareness of hegemony.[73] Kahl offers a unique look at critical assessment through a discussion of critical outcomes rather than just assessment methods that promote student participation in the assessment process. This is

71. Brew and Riley, "Measuring Student Support for Participative Assessment and Related Strategies," 47.

72. Keesing-Styles, "The Relationship Between Critical Pedagogy and Assessment in Teacher Education," 16.

73. Kahl, "Critical Communication Pedagogy and Assessment."

an important article for any critical educator and may help us to consider how to create critically focused courses in the future. One of the biggest takeaways from Kahl is his belief that students should be assessed in the same way that they learned. So, if concepts were taught through small group dialogue, they should be assessed in the same way.[74] This, of course, may be more difficult in one-shot instruction or even short-term information literacy credit courses.

Kahl is not the only educator discussing student journals as an assessment method in higher education. Jennifer Moon has written extensively on the advantages of reflective writing. She advocates developing assessment criteria in conjunction with reflective curriculum in order to thoughtfully develop ways to measure student learning through reflection.[75] She goes on to note that when reflective activities are used as a "means of learning," they can be assessed through traditional methods. However, "more interesting issues arise when the purpose of reflective work is that learners improve their ability to learn from reflection."[76] In writing about reflection in a management and spirituality course, Kathryn Pavlovich notes how difficult reflective journals can be for students, because they require students to express ideas using their personal voice.[77] However, Pavlovich asserts that students can achieve reflective practice through journaling if there are clear guidelines for how the journals are assessed.[78]

In her book, Reale writes that "when reflection works, *practice happens before theory*, and students begin to trust their own perceptions and take an active part in their own learning."[79] While far less prevalent, subjective assessments such as learning journals are also seen in the information literacy classroom. In a project that

74. Kahl, "Critical Communication Pedagogy and Assessment," 2619.

75. Moon, *A Handbook of Reflective and Experiential Learning*, 155.

76. Moon, *A Handbook of Reflective and Experiential Learning*, 155.

77. Kathryn Pavlovich, "The Development of Reflective Practice through Student Journals," *Higher Education Research & Development* 26, no. 3 (2007): 289.

78. Pavlovich, "The Development of Reflective Practice through Student Journals," 293.

79. Reale, Becoming a Reflective Librarian and Teacher, 96.

included multiple assessment methods, Claire McGuinness and Michelle Brien explored the use of reflective research journals to (1) keep students on track with their research goals, and (2) assess students' understanding and application of the research topics discussed in class.[80] They discuss how the reflective writings of the students "tell the stories behind the letter grades, describing how initial confusion slowly gives way to increasing engagement with individual research topics and a growing sense of confidence in one's ability to do effective research."[81] In their assessment work, Jackie Belanger, Rebecca Bliquez, and Sharleen Mondal found that the qualitative information garnered from students' reflective writing brought the voices of their students to a more prominent position in their assessment practices.[82]

Feminist assessment practices ask students to "reveal what is important to them, what they want to learn, and where their needs are not being met."[83] One way this is done is through assessment techniques that rely on dialogue between teacher and student.[84] These are assessments that "value listening over looking, connection over separation, and thinking together over counting responses."[85] This can be seen through approaches that value voice and listening, such as focus groups and portfolio assessments. Focus groups, small group interviews between students and a teacher/facilitator, seek student voice and validate student knowledge through dialogue.[86]

---

80. Claire McGuinness and Michelle Brien, "Using Reflective Journals to Assess the Research Process," *Reference Services Review* 35, no. 1 (2007): 31.

81. McGuinness and Brien, "Using Reflective Journals to Assess the Research Process," 32.

82. Jackie Belanger, Rebecca Bliquez, and Sharleen Mondal, "Developing a Collaborative Faculty-Librarian Information Literacy Assessment Project," *Library Review* 61, no. 2 (2012): 68-91.

83. Joan Poliner Shapiro, "What is Feminist Assessment?" in *Students at the Center: Feminist Assessment*, ed. Caryn McTighe Musil (Washington, D.C.: Association of American Colleges, 1992), 31.

84. Jennifer Foley, "Using Feminist Pedagogy to Create Meaningful Assessment for Learning in One-Shot Library Sessions," (Presented at Southeastern Library Assessment Conference, Atlanta, GA, November 2017).

85. Shapiro, "What is Feminist Assessment?" 34.

86. Accardi, *Feminist Pedagogy for Library Instruction*, 87.

The portfolio as an alternative assessment technique "values process in addition to product, provides space for student expression, and challenges traditional teacher/student relations by empowering students to choose how to represent themselves for evaluation."[87] As a collection of student work over time, portfolios can be an important way to demonstrate student learning and growth through multiple projects and self-reflection. According to Pat Hutchings, student portfolios demonstrate a student's learning journey, expose how students make meaning, and promote dialogue.[88] Accardi identifies these as the most suitable assessment methods for library instruction programs that center on one-shot instruction sessions.[89]

A Note about Assessing Value in Libraries

The literature is rife with questions about how critical pedagogy and assessment can work together.[90] The conversation about the compatibility of CIL and assessment is in line with the continuous debate in higher education about accountability versus improvement. Reflecting after years of living in this dichotomy, Peter Ewell stated:

> I was convinced 20 years ago that widespread institutional attention to designing robust assessment-for-improvement programs and to taking visible action based on evidence from these programs

87. Accardi, *Feminist Pedagogy for Library Instruction*, 85.

88. Pat Hutchings, "Learning Over Time: Portfolio Assessment," *AAHE Bulletin* 42 (1990): quoted in Caryn McTighe Musil, ed., *Students at the Center: Feminist Assessment* (Washington, D.C.: Association of American Colleges, 1992), 55.

89. Maria T. Accardi, "Teaching Against the Grain: Critical Assessment in the Library Classroom," in *Critical Library Instruction: Theories and Methods*, eds. Maria T. Accardi, Emily Drabinski, and Alana Kumbier (Duluth, MN: Library Juice Press, 2010), 251-64.

90. Gregory and Higgins, "Reorienting an Information Literacy Program Toward Social Justice"; Gardner and Halpern, "At Odds with Assessment"; Benjamin Harris and Anne Jumonville, "Assessment is Dead, Long Live Assessment: Considering the Risks of Engaged Critical Pedagogy," (paper, Annual Conference of the Canadian Association of Professional Academic Librarians, University of Ottawa, Ottawa, ON, May 2015). We obtained the original script for this presentation from the authors and cite from that manuscript; and Graf and Harris, "Reflective Assessment."

would be sufficient to provide accountability—and would obviate the need to report measures of student achievement that can be benchmarked or compared. I do not believe this today. We will need to do both in the coming years, buying the necessary time to accomplish the more needed and desirable task of building institutional infrastructures for evidence-based continuous improvement with public performance reporting.[91]

Taking Ewell's comment to heart, it is essential that we continue to engage in conversations about value in academic libraries,[92] because we must (even if we don't like it) provide administrators with data when requested. We can refuse to give the provost data about retention and graduation rates, but in making that choice we risk not having a classroom to do the work that matters. And, "if we, as librarians and critical educators, are not engaging in any research that demonstrates 'value', our administrations and universities will have those conversations for us (and without us)."[93] Therefore, we must "recognize the importance of libraries demonstrating value to those who determine our funding levels"[94] while striking a better balance "between assessment focused on improvement and research focused on accountability."[95]

It is clear from the literature on assessment practice that instruction librarians are doing good work in assessing student learning.[96] Because instruction librarians are already engaged in

91. Peter Ewell, "Assessment, Accountability, and Improvement: Revising the Tension," (Occasional Paper #1, National Institute for Learning Outcomes Assessment (NILOA), University of Illinois and Indiana University, Urbana, IL, November 2009), 20, http://www.learningoutcomeassessment.org/documents/PeterEwell_005.pdf.

92. Meagan Oakleaf, "What's the Value of an Academic Library? The Development of the ACRL Value of Academic Libraries Comprehensive Research Review and Report," *Australian Academic & Research Libraries* 42, no. 1 (2011): 1-13.

93. Megan Oakleaf, "Do the Right (Write) Thing: Engaging in Academic Library Value Research," *College and Research Libraries* 72, no. 3 (2011): 204-206, cited in Gardner and Halpern, "At Odds with Assessment," 47.

94. Meredith Farkas, "Accountability vs. Improvement: Seeking Balance in the Value of Academic Libraries Initiative," *OLA Quarterly* 19, no. 1 (2013): 6.

95. Farkas, "Accountability vs. Improvement," 6.

96. Erlinger, "Outcomes Assessment."

this work, it is to the benefit of our libraries that we bring this expertise into value assessment projects. For those of us who want value research to be more meaningful, we can help our library to demonstrate value while helping to diversify the types of data collection methods used in this research. In doing so, we can provide a more robust picture to administrators about the value of our libraries to the campus and to the students, faculty, and staff who use them.

Wrap-Up

We see an inherent similarity between critical pedagogy and assessment in that they both support hope for the future and progress towards positive change. Assessment is essential for pedagogical growth and meaningful student learning. In this chapter we provided an overview of how to approach assessment through a critical lens, which includes centering the student experience by opening up dialogue, sharing roles and responsibilities, and negotiating curriculum and assessment. We expand on these assessment strategies in the following chapters by providing examples of how we've incorporated these into our own work. In chapter three, we provide examples of teaching assessment and in chapter four we discuss real world implementations of inclusive student learning assessment techniques.

Chapter 3

ASSESSMENT OF TEACHING

Continual assessment of teaching is essential to professional growth. It requires reflection on practice, including the ways that we design and deliver curricula and how we interact with students. Assessing teaching can be time consuming, daunting, and disheartening. Nevertheless, assessing ourselves leads to reflection, and the benefits gained from reflecting on our practice far outweigh the negatives. As Carolyn Gardner and Rebecca Halpern note: "every time we reflect on an educational interaction, from a tutorial, to a one-shot session, to a semester-long class, we put ourselves in the learner's position, solve problems, and grow as teachers."[1] Stewart asserts that to engage in critical-inclusive pedagogy, educators must first "do the self-work needed and the recognition of being the oppressor, with the responsibility to constantly question and act against systems of oppression."[2] The assessment methods discussed in this chapter include teaching reflection journals, peer observation, Critical Friends Groups, and face-to-face student feedback. These methods map to all tenets of the Critical-Inclusive Pedagogical Framework (CIPF), as seen in **Figure 2**. Throughout the chapter, we offer our own experiences with these methods and share the voices of others who have engaged with us in this work.

---

1. Gardner and Halpern, "At Odds with Assessment," 47.

2. Stewart, "Advancing a Critical and Inclusive Praxis," 19.

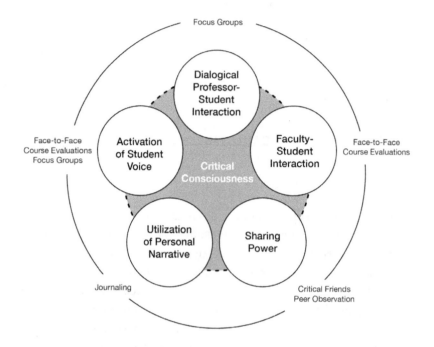

Figure 2: Assessment of Teaching Mapped to the CIPF

Self-Reflection & Peer Observation

Journaling

One of the ways we began our journey into critical assessment was through the practice of reflective writing. The journals we use to reflect on our teaching are informal personal records of every class we teach, logged directly after individual information literacy sessions. They vary from hand-written notebooks to digital journals, but they always demonstrate personal critiques of lesson plans, teaching methods, and observed student reactions to course content. Requiring no real training and only a minimal commitment of time and effort,[3] journaling is now an integral part of our teaching practice. Through critical reflection, we can make important observations that lead to more effective curricula and teaching practices that are responsive to student needs.

Overview & Implementation

Admittedly, we do not follow a formal journaling format, such as those outlined in the writings of Reale or Moon.[4] Some of our reflections consist of notes jotted on our printed lesson plans or scribbled on a sticky-note. Regardless of how it's done, it is essential to integrate the practice of journaling into your everyday routine. There are multiple reasons to implement journals into your practice, but if your aim is to use journaling as an assessment tool, then identifying areas for improvement is the primary purpose. When first beginning, you may feel comfortable simply recounting what happened in a specific information literacy session. While this practice may be fun, relaxing, or even cathartic, it doesn't necessarily provide any practical information that you can use to improve your practice. As you can see from the examples in **Figure 3** and **Figure 4**, these journal entries show thoughts and feelings recounted with no actual reflection; here, we did not push ourselves to reflect critically. Why did we feel "preachy" when discussing race, sex, and class in publishing? A deeper reflection would have led to a critical examination of our own identity and privilege. Why was it good that students discussed police brutality in the context of Rodney King? In this particular class it was good because these students are Criminal Justice majors, many of whom will be police officers; it was significant that they wanted to discuss police brutality. However, this journal entry doesn't go beyond recounting the details of the class discussion. There is no

---

3. We realize "minimal" is subjective. We also admit that we did have to work to find the time in our schedules for reflection when we started. Now we block thirty minutes a day for reflection, usually directly after a class session.

4. Reale, *Becoming a Reflective Librarian and Teacher;* and Jennifer Moon, *Learning Journals: A Handbook for Reflective Practice and Professional Development* (2nd ed, London: Routledge, 2004).

processing about changing practice, changing our approach, or improving the lesson plan.

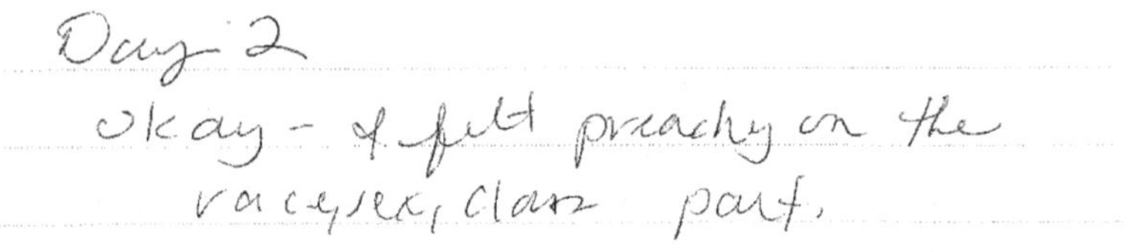

Day 2
okay - of felt preachy on the
race/sex, class part.

Figure 3: Journal Excerpt Recounting Personal Feelings

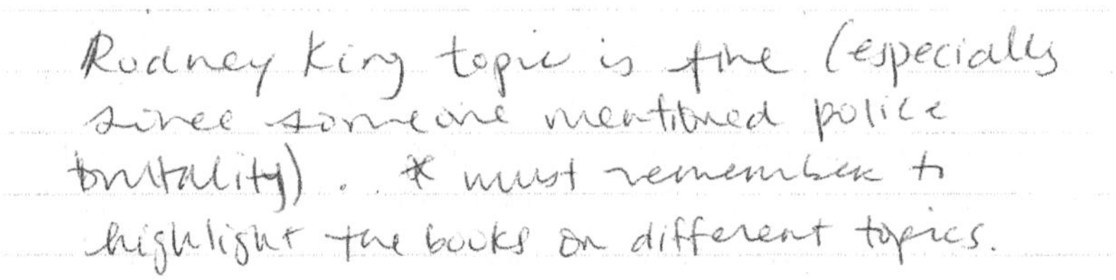

Rodney King topic is fine (especially
since someone mentioned police
brutality). * must remember to
highlight the books on different topics.

Figure 4: Journal Excerpt Recounting Class Discussion

It took time for us to understand how to reflect critically on our practices. We found that the more we read about reflection, the more we improved our own reflective writing. We started to dig deeper and write with an intent to improve our teaching. This involves asking not only what, but also why, and then examining how those decisions influenced others in the classroom. **Figure 5** and **Figure 6** show movement towards greater reflection and questioning of our practice.

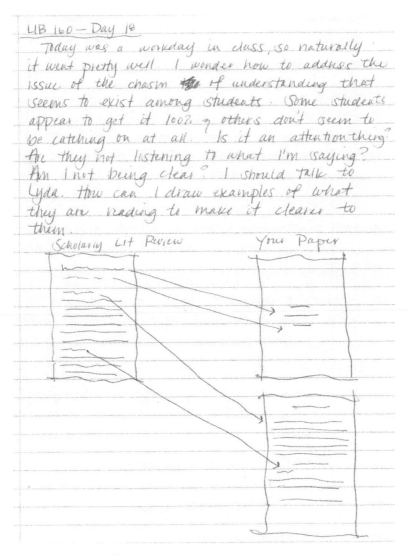

LIB 160 – Day 18

Today was a workday in class, so naturally
it went pretty well. I wonder how to address the
issue of the chasm ~~the~~ of understanding that
seems to exist among students. Some students
appear to get it 100% & others don't seem to
be catching on at all. Is it an attention thing?
Are they not listening to what I'm saying?
Am I not being clear? I should talk to
Lyda. How can I draw examples of what
they are reading to make it clearer to
them.

Scholarly Lit Review   Your Paper

Figure 5: Journal with Critical Reflection

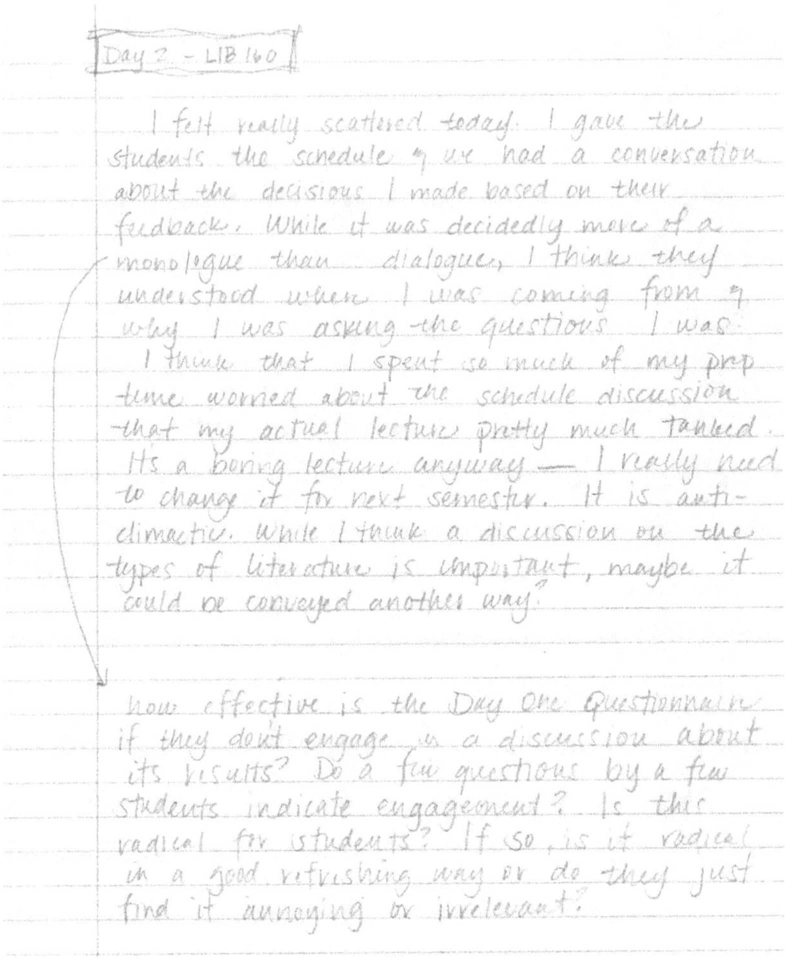

Day 2 - LIB 160

I felt really scattered today. I gave the
students the schedule + we had a conversation
about the decisions I made based on their
feedback. While it was decidedly more of a
monologue than dialogue, I think they
understood where I was coming from +
why I was asking the questions I was.
   I think that I spent so much of my prep
time worried about the schedule discussion
that my actual lecture pretty much tanked.
Its a boring lecture anyway — I really need
to change it for next semester. It is anti-
climactic. While I think a discussion on the
types of literature is important, maybe it
could be conveyed another way.

how effective is the Day One Questionnaire
if they don't engage in a discussion about
its results? Do a few questions by a few
students indicate engagement? Is this
radical for students? If so, is it radical
in a good refreshing way or do they just
find it annoying or irrelevant?

Figure 6: Revisiting Reflective Journal Entry

Teaching reflection journals provide a record of the decisions
we make in the classroom. They inform future pedagogical
decisions and serve as indicators of effective teaching methods.
While disciplining ourselves to get started with teaching reflection

journals was difficult, now we can't imagine teaching without them. We are constantly referring to our journals when planning one-shot lesson plans or reorganizing our credit courses for the next semester. We also share our journals with each other, which provides insight into how each of us is approaching certain topics or dealing with issues in the classroom. Our journals give us the ability to look back after a long semester and know we are making informed decisions about improving teaching and learning. The most significant benefit of the journals is that we can see patterns in our teaching over time. Looking back over multiple semesters of journals allows us to assess persistent issues with our practice.

Tips & Best Practices

After reflecting on our own experience, we have come up with a set of recommendations for librarians hoping to implement teaching reflection journals:

- Set aside a dedicated period for initial reflection. This is crucial. Schedule 15-30 minutes after every class period to journal. We schedule this on our calendar to ensure no one sets a meeting over this time.
- Revisit your journal. Separation from the actual event upon which you are reflecting can be helpful for deeper critical reflection. For example, when reflecting on a challenge, consider a solution in your journal and then revisit that solution later to see if your thinking has changed over time.
- Use your journal to inform curricular decisions. Using journals for assessment means that the journal is your data. Before you sit down to plan that next one-shot, re-read your reflection of the last time you taught the session. This allows you to remember what worked and what did not.
- Share your journal with a trusted peer and engage in a dialogue with them about your thinking.

Peer Observation

Overview & Implementation

Peer observation is another method of assessment that we have passionately adopted as a way to improve our teaching. Departmental, and even institutional, support for peer observation is important to its success. Supportive colleagues and a healthy culture of assessment bolster collaborative assessment practices.[5] In this section, we discuss three different peer observation initiatives: peer observation done as a committee, cross-institutional peer observation, and cross-departmental peer observation as implemented in our own library. The experiences are built upon the best practices for peer observation in libraries as outlined by Jaena Alabi and William Weare,[6] as well as the twelve tips for successful peer observation in a college setting discussed by Zarrin Siddiqui, Diana Jonas-Dwyer, and Sandra Carr.[7] While both articles discuss tips for peer observation, the major takeaways are the importance of confidentiality and effective communication between the observer and the observed. We encourage anyone setting up a peer observation program in their library to begin their conversations with these two pieces.

We began peer observation as an initiative in our library's Curriculum Committee, a group tasked with the oversight and assessment of library credit courses. Our goals were to build collegiality and trust between committee members and to develop

---

5. The concept of a culture of assessment within academic libraries has been widely explored by authors including Meredith Gorran Farkas and Lisa Janicke Hinchliffe. We suggest the following articles: Meredith G. Farkas, "Building and Sustaining a Culture of Assessment: Best Practices for Change Leadership," *Reference Services Review* 41, no. 1 (2013): 13-31; Meredith G. Farkas and Lisa J. Hinchliffe, "Library Faculty and Instructional Assessment: Creating a Culture of Assessment through the High Performance Programming Model of Organizational Transformation," *Collaborative Librarianship* 5, no. 3 (2013): 177; and Meredith G. Farkas, Lisa J. Hinchliffe, and Amy H. Houk, "Bridges and Barriers: Factors Influencing a Culture of Assessment in Academic Libraries," *College & Research Libraries* 76, no. 2 (2015): 150-169.

6. Alabi and Weare, "Peer Review of Teaching."

7. Zarrin Seema Siddiqui, Diana Jonas-Dwyer, and Sandra E. Carr, "Twelve Tips for Peer Observation of Teaching," *Medical Teacher* 29, no. 4 (2007): 297-300.

a way to assess teaching outside of course evaluations. We began by exploring the literature on peer observation of teaching in both the higher education and library literatures. From this literature review, we determined our process and developed guidelines (see **Appendix A**). We followed the model of pre-meeting, observation, and post-meeting.[8] Additionally, we included a required face-to-face student feedback session for each credit course as we discuss later in this chapter. We made sure to stress in our documents that peer observation is used to improve teaching and learning and is non-evaluative. Any documentation from the peer observation, such as observer-written comments, was confidential and was excluded from annual faculty evaluations.

Peer observation with the committee took place between spring and fall of 2016. At the end of fall 2016, after going through two peer observation sessions with two different partners, we decided to seek the perspective of librarians outside of the committee. Ultimately, we sought the perspectives of librarians outside of our institution so that we could get feedback on our teaching from people who were not involved in our day-to-day practice. After finding our partner institution, we held a retreat so we could meet each other and discuss the peer observation project. This retreat was a way to build camaraderie among the librarians, and to make sure that everyone involved had a voice in the development of the process. We used the original Curriculum Committee documents as a jumping-off point and updated them at the retreat so that they met the needs of all participating librarians. We also developed an idea checklist that outlined possible areas of teaching that could be observed, such as delivery, pace, or student participation (see **Appendix B**). After these initial discussions, we selected partners and got acquainted with them over lunch, learning about liaison areas and teaching obligations. These collaborative peer observations took place over one academic year. Despite the amount of coordination involved in this inter-institutional project,

---

8. Martin and Double, "Developing Higher Education Teaching Skills through Peer Observation and Collaborative Reflection," 161-170.

the overall take-away was positive. Observing and being observed by peers outside of our library forced us to examine issues about our practice that had not been seen in peer observation within our committee. We are now involved in cross-departmental peer observation in our own library as part of the work of all liaison librarians, following the same process outlined in **Appendix A**. This indicates a significant shift toward a culture of assessment in our organization.

Although being observed in the classroom prompted moments of vulnerability and apprehension, the experiences have had lasting benefits for our teaching practice. We gained a greater awareness of how we physically move around our classrooms, learned how to incorporate collaborative tools more effectively into our teaching, and adopted new approaches for engaging students in class discussions. Working with peers, especially those outside of your own organization, can help you see your teaching in new ways. To see how in-depth this feedback can be, we provide an example of peer observation notes in **Appendix C**.

Because peer observation is a collaboration, we invited our colleagues to share some of their experiences:

> A major theme that developed from the peer observations and subsequent discussions with my partner was the relationship between our teaching persona and our identity and personality outside the classroom. We noted how challenging it can be to project both confidence and approachability. It was a great opportunity to discuss our feelings about our teaching practices and identities as educators in a safe, non-judgmental space.

> I like observing others teach because it reminds me that there isn't one right way to teach and that a variety of methods are effective depending on what you are hoping students will learn. I also feel like I gain a lot from being able to sit in the back of the room and observe what students are doing throughout the class. I'm somehow always surprised to see that students are paying attention. Sure, you get the occasional student who is doing something else, but the overwhelming majority are listening, following along, and doing their best to learn something.

The biggest challenges were around scheduling: one department taught nearly all credit-bearing classes in eight weeks, while the other department taught one-shots that were scattered about in the semester. This, combined with the geographical and weather issues that winter in the Rocky Mountains presents, led to some observations not getting scheduled. It was also tough to make one's colleagues do things like respond to emails from their partners if they did not report to you. Lastly, some pairs were able to establish trust quickly, but others just didn't gel. As the article we chose as our common reading pointed out, establishing trust for peer review of teaching is important, and it is easier to do when you work with people every day.

Observing someone from another library teach—as opposed to attending a presentation/panel at a conference—is a fairly rare experience, and I took away a lot of energizing ideas and approaches from my observation partner. I also appreciated the insights that my partner offered me to improve both my lesson plan as well as my delivery. They differed in some respects from the feedback that I had already received from members of my own department, and I appreciated this different perspective/viewpoint.

These reflections highlight the value of peer observation as well as the challenge of trying to connect both personally and professionally with others. We believe it is important to start any peer observation process with librarians or disciplinary faculty from your own organization before collaborating with a different institution.

Tips & Best Practices

After reflecting on our experience, we have a set of recommendations for librarians hoping to implement peer observation:

- Read the literature broadly before starting so you make the right decisions for your team.

- Consider doing peer observation as a team initiative. This makes it part of the team/committee goals and helps to create a culture of assessment in your library.
- Seek partners from different institutions. Going outside your library is beneficial because you gain perspective outside the culture of your own instruction program. Consider distance if you are planning to work with peers outside your library. Our peers were two hours away, which meant a lot of driving for everyone involved.
- Ensure that everyone has a voice in creating the peer observation process and guidelines.
- Do not include peer observation reports as part of an evaluation process.
- Reflect on your observation experiences.

Critical Friends Group

Overview & Implementation

The Critical Friends Group (CFG) model is a collaborative method of assessment that combines peer observation and dialogue with self-reflection and self-assessment. We've found the CFG to be an effective way for liaison librarians to collaborate with disciplinary faculty on improving curricula and teaching. We see participating in a CFG as compatible with a critical practice, because it pushes us to share power with our peers. We share power by opening ourselves up to critique. We put ourselves into the role of learner, with the understanding that there is still much we don't know about teaching and that there is always room for improvement. Being a critical friend requires that we trust in each other and mutually commit to improvement. Not only do you have to be willing to accept critical feedback from peers, you must be willing to make changes based on that feedback.

Our experience implementing a CFG to improve one of our credit courses resulted in significant curriculum changes and more participatory teaching methods. We first implemented a CFG when students in one of our credit courses, *LIB 160: Criminal Justice Library Research*, were having trouble writing research questions, a skill needed in upper division Criminology & Criminal Justice research methods courses. In an effort to improve our lesson plan and to ensure that students were able to transfer their skills from *LIB 160* into upper division Criminology courses, we reached out to a faculty member in Criminology for feedback. To start the CFG, we sent the faculty member the lesson plans for the two-day lesson on research questions and asked that she observe two class sessions in order to provide feedback on the lesson plans, content, and teaching. After the first class, we discussed updates to the lesson plan and vocabulary that was important for students in later Criminology courses, such as a conversation on dependent and independent variables. After the second class, the three of us discussed organization of the two-day lesson plan and made significant changes to the order in which the two lesson plans appear in the scheme of the course, as well as ways to improve the in-class activities. Using this feedback, we updated the lesson plan. You can see the full range of changes in the journal excerpt in **Figure 7**.

A couple of weeks following the observation sessions, we met with the faculty member again to go over the lesson plan changes. This morphed into a larger conversation about the placement of *LIB 160* within the Criminology major. Our discussion prompted a proposal to make the library course a co-requisite with a writing-intensive Criminology course, *CRJ 380: Justice Research & Statistics.*[9] This change was approved by the Criminology faculty in fall 2017 and will be in effect starting in fall 2018. This curriculum change would not have happened without the honest and constructive dialogue of the CFG. The group will restructure in fall 2018 to include all *LIB 160* and *CRJ 380* instructors.

Engaging in reflective writing after a post-observation discussion can help you process the comments of your peer.

---

9. Up to fall 2018 LIB 160 was a required course in the Criminology major that students could take at any time.

The journal entry in **Figure 7** is an example of critical reflection following a peer observation session. When we went back to this journal entry days later, we were able to reflect on our own practice more critically based on peer feedback.

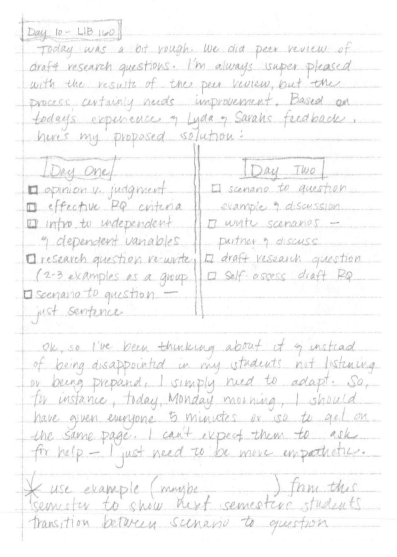

Figure 7: Critical Reflection Following Peer Observation

Our experience with the CFG model was rewarding. Not only did we improve our lesson plan on writing research questions, we made significant curriculum changes in both the library and Criminology programs. Inviting a non-librarian into our classroom pushed us out of our comfort zone, as neither of us had ever been observed by a non-library faculty member. Having a disciplinary faculty member ask questions about pedagogical choices pushed us to reflect more critically on our approach to teaching information literacy. This also reinforced the teaching role of librarians on our campus. Most importantly, the CFG let us develop a stronger collegial relationship between library and disciplinary faculty. The Criminology faculty member also found the CFG model helpful, as can be seen in her reflection on the process:

> Watching another instructor teach material (on how to develop a research question), which serves as the foundation for material I teach in a Research Methods course gave me a much better understanding of students' background and preparation for the content and assignments in my own course. It made me realize that I need to find other opportunities to learn about the content in the other courses that students take before my course, either by asking students about their level of preparation or by talking to or observing other faculty. In addition, I also learned new approaches to content delivery. For instance, the instructor asked students to revise a poorly developed research question in pairs and then write their revised research questions on the white board for the class to consider and discuss. I found this technique to provide a nice way to engage students and cover many examples of research questions in one course meeting.

Tips & Best Practices

After reflecting on our experience, we have a set of recommendations for librarians hoping to implement a Critical Friends Group:

- Start with a specific goal. Consider the teaching question you want your CFG to focus on as they observe your teaching.

- Meet first to discuss the lesson plan. We believe meeting before the classes to discuss the lesson plan is helpful for providing context for the group.
- Meet immediately after any observation to discuss the class session.
- Take time to reflect on the observation and to formulate constructive feedback for the next discussion.
- Have multiple meetings following the observation. This provides time to reflect on initial reactions and can result in more productive dialogue within your group.

Face-to-Face Feedback[10]

We find asking students for feedback to be an essential task for centering student voice in the classroom. We gather direct feedback from our students as often as possible. We've implemented face-to-face feedback for credit courses through verbal course evaluations and in one-shot instruction through focus groups. Both of these methods allow us to use student voice to make curricular changes and improve our teaching. Developing a dialogue with our students about their classroom experience has made face-to-face feedback one of the most meaningful ways we assess our teaching.

Face-to-Face Course Evaluations

Overview & Implementation

Face-to-face course evaluations are a form of course evaluation that takes place face-to-face instead of through an anonymous evaluation form. It is a discussion with the entire class instead of individual students. We find that this method is not only useful for getting in-depth answers from students related to our classroom

10. Michael Oravitz, Kristin Bovaird-Abbo, and Karen Hessler, "Just Ask: Enriching Evaluation through Face-to-Face Student Feedback," (Presentation at the Center for Enhancement of Teaching and Learning, University of Northern Colorado, 2015), https://digscholarship.unco.edu/tla/24/.

teaching, but is a valuable exercise in centering student voice in the assessment of teaching. We avoid "how's my driving"[11] type questions that focus on things about the instructor (such as preparation, communication skills, or interpersonal relationships), since these things may be difficult to discuss in person. Instead, we focus on questions that are about classroom teaching. Examples of these questions are:

- What about this class did you find most beneficial as a student/researcher?
- Is there any part of this class you felt was extraneous or irrelevant?
- If you could change anything about this class for future students, what would it be?

Face-to-face course evaluation allows us to ask meaningful questions and provides us with an opportunity to follow-up in the moment. Instead of a Likert Scale question that asks a student to rate interest in the course, face-to-face feedback asks about topics students found most and least engaging. We can then probe deeper with students about updating course content. This helps improve teaching by letting us retain what did work and discard what didn't work in the classroom. The best part of face-to-face feedback is the conversation students have with each other. When discussing helpful assignments, for example, students discover that while one person found an assignment unhelpful for learning, another student found it very helpful. This provides a teaching moment for the students as they gain a new perspective. For a complete example of face-to-face course evaluation data, see **Appendix D**.

We began face-to-face course evaluation in fall 2016 as an initiative of our library Curriculum Committee. It takes place in the last week of the course, usually in the final twenty to thirty minutes of the class. To prepare, each instructor develops questions that are

---

11. Oravitz, Bovaird-Abbo, and Hessler, "Just Ask."

specific to their course. If an instructor has implemented a new assignment or activity, or organized the course in a new way, they will usually ask for feedback about these changes in their questions. Many of the questions are broad and seek feedback about course organization, timing of assignments, clarity of instructions, and use of class time.

In our process, the course instructor does not facilitate the face-to-face course evaluation; we select partners for this process. We made this decision thinking that students might be more honest if they were not speaking to the person who taught the class. The facilitator takes notes during the discussion and then types them up and sends the feedback to the instructor after final grades are submitted. The pair then meet to discuss the face-to-face feedback and talk through possible curriculum changes. While the results are confidential and do not appear in any evaluation materials, faculty are encouraged to discuss feedback with the Curriculum Committee Chair if they are concerned or have questions about how to use the feedback to make improvements.

For us, face-to-face course evaluation is the most valuable way to evaluate a course. Students take this face-to-face feedback session very seriously, offering honest and constructive criticism. The dialogue developed between the students and the facilitator is so much richer than the anonymous snippets students leave in written course evaluations. While the feedback from students is still confidential, the facilitator can contextualize the comments and ask students for more clarification. For example, if a student mentions something about inconsistent grading practices, the facilitator can ask that student to elaborate on what they meant by inconsistent and ask the rest of the students if they share the same concern. Students often build off of each other's comments and continue the conversation among themselves with few interjections from the facilitator. This type of direct and specific feedback is invaluable in curriculum development. Additionally, the facilitator has the autonomy to reword questions if something is confusing for students or if the original question is not eliciting a response.

Another benefit is the conversation that happens after the session between the instructor and the facilitator. Ideally, the facilitator will be a teaching librarian who is familiar with the goals and values of the instruction program. After hearing what the students have to say, the instructor and facilitator can discuss the feedback and use it to make positive change to content and pedagogical approach.

Face-to-face course evaluations have helped us to make real change in our practices. Other Curriculum Committee members share their appreciation for the process below:

> I appreciated hearing student voices in the face-to-face feedback a colleague collected for me. They brought up issues that were not covered in the official course evaluations. I also valued the chance to ask specific questions that were not included on the formal evaluations.

> Face-to-face feedback has been more useful for suggesting concrete changes to my courses than standard course evaluations ever were. I've gotten fewer of "the girl was condescending" comments, which makes getting the results back less emotionally taxing.

Tips & Best Practices

After reflecting on our experience, we have a set of recommendations for librarians hoping to implement face-to-face course evaluation:

- Be aware that not all students feel comfortable sharing their opinions in front of a group, particularly if they feel like their opinion may be unpopular among their classmates. Leave time after the session to allow anyone a chance to speak one-on-one with the facilitator. Additionally, there should always be an opportunity for anonymous course evaluations.
- Assign feedback partners at the start of a semester. If you are doing peer observation, use the same partner.

- Set aside enough class time for feedback. We recommend at least twenty minutes.
- Consider a pre- and post-meeting between instructor and facilitator in order to clarify questions and student comments.
- Face-to-face feedback can work in one-shot instruction; your partner can speak to a sample of students you taught and/or speak with instructors. Consider a time after an assignment's due-date if the one-shot is directly related to a course assignment.

Focus Groups

Overview & Implementation

Focus groups are structured group interviews that involve a facilitator and volunteer participants. Unlike the face-to-face course evaluation, focus groups combine students from multiple sections of courses or students from across campus.[12] Discussed in the literature as a feminist approach to assessment, focus groups can be an enlightening way to improve teaching.[13] This approach to assessment takes significant planning, training, organization, and people. Despite the logistics involved, the potential exists to gather meaningful assessment data with focus groups.

In fall 2017, we embarked on a focus group project that aimed to improve the content and delivery of the curriculum for our first-year English composition program. We teach approximately fifty one-shot sessions per semester for this program and were ready to freshen up the lesson plan. This project involved the Information Literacy and Undergraduate Support (ILUS) department (five faculty members and one staff member) and took nearly an entire

---

12   There is a dearth of literature about using focus groups for information literacy assessment. For a discussion of this literature, see Erlinger, "Outcomes Assessment," 449.

13   Musil, *Students at the Center.*

semester to prepare.[14] To design our focus groups, we looked outside the library literature to the work of Richard Krueger and Mary Anne Casey.[15] Their book helped us design two specific focus groups, one for first-year English students and one for instructors of first-year English (see **Appendix E**).

Conducting focus groups is a lot of work. We had trouble getting student and instructor volunteers despite multiple reminders, various opportunities to attend a focus group, and the offer of free food. We put many hours into designing, coordinating, and facilitating focus groups for a small number of participants. Despite this, we did receive valuable feedback from the students and instructors we interviewed. As with face-to-face course evaluations, one of the greatest benefits of focus groups is the conversations that participants have with each other and the facilitator. With a simple question or a short prompt, focus group participants are generally eager to share their experiences and opinions with the group. Focus groups also offer the opportunity to garner more in-depth feedback from participants. For instance, participants can be asked to write about an experience. Their narrative might encourage the writer to divulge more specific details or suggestions than a verbal comment may have provided.

Tips & Best Practices

After reflecting on our experience, we have a set of recommendations for librarians hoping to implement focus groups:

- Check with your Institutional Review Board (IRB) before you embark on any significant focus group projects, as you are working with human research subjects.
- Partner with one or more faculty or teaching assistants to get participants rather than a blanket call for participation.

14   While this was a department effort, Assistant Professor Brianne Markowski led this initiative.

15   Richard A. Krueger and Mary Anne Casey, *Focus Groups: A Practical Guide for Applied Research*, 3rd ed. (Thousand Oaks, CA.: Sage Publications, 2000).

- Design your focus group to include various types of questions. Not everyone will feel comfortable answering certain types of questions. By incorporating a variety of questions, you will have a better chance of getting everyone in your group to participate. For example, one question may ask participants to reflect on an experience and then share it with the group, while another may be a simple yes or no. Both questions can provide valuable data.
- Have a script prepared and do a practice run-through of your focus group with your colleagues to help address any awkward or unclear questions.
- Have a dedicated note-taker in each focus group. This should be someone familiar with the research, but not a formal facilitator. This frees the facilitator to lead the discussion and ask follow-up questions of the participants.
- Offer incentives as a way to get volunteers. Make sure whatever you offer is appropriate for the time and effort you are asking from your volunteers.

Wrap-Up

In this chapter we discussed methods for assessing teaching that map to the CIPF. We get feedback from peers inside and outside of our library in order to gain different perspectives on pedagogical approaches and to engage in a more critical examination of our teaching. We also strive to engage students in conversation about our teaching since they are the ones most impacted by our practice. The materials we provide in the appendices for this chapter may help to jump start your own assessment work. We hope that the excerpts from our personal journals encourage you to get started with your own teaching journal, even if you start with simply recording what happened. We also hope that sharing face-to-face feedback and peer observation notes will help alleviate some of the fear associated with asking others to critique your practice. In the next chapter we discuss approaches to assessing student learning that are mapped to the CIPF.

Chapter 4

ASSESSMENT OF STUDENT LEARNING

When we set out to write this book, we thought we could discuss typical classroom assessment techniques re-envisioned through a critical lens. After reading the work of critical pedagogues, especially those involved with assessment practice, we realized that such a discussion is not really possible. Critical assessment is bigger than that; as Keesing-Styles notes, it "involves an entirely new orientation—one that embraces a number of principles that may not be familiar in the generic assessment literature."[1] Critical assessment embraces tenets of feminist pedagogy such as being democratic and student centered, being collaborative, valuing voice, and caring about the whole student.[2] The focus is on changing our assessment practice through student self- and peer-assessment, student reflection, and student participation in classroom assessment.

As we've noted, assessment practice is one of the most political processes in higher education and traditional models can be seen as a form of exploitation or oppression. Thus, critical assessment requires us to share power with our students. This requires us to

---

1. Keesing-Styles, "The Relationship Between Critical Pedagogy and Assessment in Teacher Education," 10.

2. Foley, "Using Feminist Pedagogy to Create Meaningful Assessment for Learning in One-Shot Library Sessions," https://scholarworks.gsu.edu/cgi/viewcontent.cgi?article=1049&context=southeasternlac

examine our authoritarianism while embracing our authority.[3] We must acknowledge that the authoritarianism granted to us by our institutions is not the same as the authority granted to us by our education and experiences. Freire argues that there is a beautiful and necessary tension between authority and freedom—navigating this tension should be continuous to ensure that we "never, never transform[s] authority into authoritarianism."[4] In this chapter, we provide a discussion of how we are implementing assessment practice in our classrooms. **Figure 8** illustrates how we've mapped our assessment practices to the CIPF.

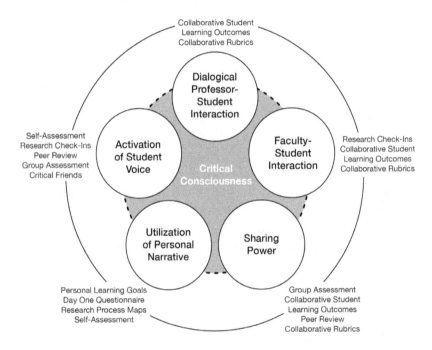

Figure 8: Assessment Mapped to CIPF

3. Joshua Beatty, "Reading Freire for First-World Librarians" (Presented at Annual Conference of the Canadian Association of Professional Academic Librarians, University of Ottawa, Ottawa, ON, May 2015).

4. Ira Shor and Paulo Freire, *A Pedagogy for Liberation: Dialogues on Transforming Education* (South Hadley, MA.: Bergin & Garvey, 1987), 90-91.

Self-Reflection

By implementing reflective activities throughout our curriculum, we hope to share with our students the value of self-reflection. Discussions in the literature about using reflection for assessment tend to apply rubrics to assess thinking.[5] We avoid using rubrics to assess reflection; for us it is counterintuitive to assess someone's own thinking process. We see self-reflection as a way to get students thinking about their research process, questioning their choices, and thinking about their own knowledge gaps and needs. We use student self-reflection to engage in dialogue with our students, offering suggestions on their process and addressing concerns they pose in their writing.

Personal Learning Goals

Students have a lot to say about their own learning—teachers just tend not to always listen. A great reflection exercise is to have students reflect on their own personal learning goals. This is a good exercise for both credit courses and one-shot instruction, and works especially well if you are involving students in creating learning outcomes and/or lesson plans. Knowing students' learning goals is essential to creating a course or session that meets their needs. Asking students to determine their own goals is quite simple: we just ask what they want from the course. Here is a personal learning goal prompt from a credit course we taught in spring 2018:

> Discuss the top three things you want out of LIB 160 this semester. These can be research-related skills, concepts, or knowledge areas. For example, you may want to gain skills in APA style or you may want to get better at selecting relevant sources.

---

5. Sarah L. Ash, Patti H. Clayton, and Maxine P. Atkinson, "Integrating Reflection and Assessment to Capture and Improve Student Learning," *Michigan Journal of Community Service Learning* 11, no. 2 (2005), 49-60, http://hdl.handle. net/2027/spo.3239521.0011.204; and Steven Jones, *Using Reflection for Assessment* (Iowa City, IA: The University of Iowa Division of Student Life), https:// vp.studentlife.uiowa.edu/assets/Using-Reflection-for-Assessment.pdf.

Responses to this prompt included "get better at organizing the evidence found from my sources"; "I want to be able not [to] struggle so much while trying to narrow my research topic"; and "be more time efficient and detailed in my research." While we had a shell schedule created for this course, the student responses prompted changes to the final schedule. We went over the schedule in detail on the second day of class, discussing how each day's lessons, activities, and assignments mapped to the students' personal learning goals. When handing out the course schedule, we showed students how their responses mapped to the overall course goals (see **Appendix F**). We also made it a point during each class session to stress how the day's activities mapped to their own goals.

The best advice we have for implementing personal learning goals is—don't do it if you won't use it! Don't ask students to tell you what they need and then toss their needs to the side without using them to develop your course content. If you want to engage students in any phase of course development, you should listen to, and act on, what they have to say. Setting personal learning goals can work in one-shots just as well as credit courses. While you can discuss learning goals at the start of a one-shot, it works best if students develop their goals a couple of days before class. You can then focus your lesson plan on the top two or three learning goals for that class.

Day One Questionnaire[6]

Similar to personal learning goals, the Day One Questionnaire (DOQ) is designed to seek and respect student objectives and preferences and is used for course development. This technique is based on the writing of Shor and reflects his desire to get students involved in course development from day one.[7] As the name

---

6. For a detailed description of our experience with Day One Questionaire, see Dineen and McCartin, "An Unfinished Journey."

7. Shor argues that "to establish the learning process as a cultural forum or public sphere for the negotiations of meanings, it helps to get students' thoughts and feelings into the open as soon as possible." Shor, *When Students Have Power*, 34.

suggests, the DOQ is a short survey given to students on the first day of instruction. We have used the DOQ to gather student input on course content as well as learning preferences. The questions we ask are:

1. What do you hope to take away from this course?
2. When it comes to research for a writing assignment, when do you feel most confident?
3. In what ways do you feel you learn best?
4. In what ways do you prefer to receive feedback?

For each question, students are given a series of answers and asked to rank them based on their preferences (see **Appendix G**). There are also open-text fields so that students can elaborate on any of their responses or provide answers not listed. By asking students to rank their preferences, we can make decisions about things like teaching approaches and how much time to spend on certain skills or concepts before finalizing the syllabus.

Recently, we modified the DOQ for a one-shot instruction session. We composed a short questionnaire asking students to consider their previous library experience and then rank a series of information literacy concepts and skills depending on what they felt they needed to learn or review. We also provided an open-text field asking students to include any skills or concepts that we might have left off the list. We used this student feedback to develop the lesson plan. We feel this is a great example of centering student voice, since the lesson plan focused on what students wanted and excluded multiple concepts that the course instructor wanted to include in the session.[8]

We have given the DOQ to our students for multiple semesters. Each time we do, we learn more about how to solicit this type of

---

8. We informed the Art & Design faculty member that we were sending a survey to students to determine the session content. We got no push back on this from the faculty member and moved forward with a successful session. It is important to note that the success of using the DOQ depends on your relationship with the faculty member and trust you've built over time.

input from students in a genuine and meaningful way. We believe that being open with your students about why they are doing the questionnaire is crucial for its success. Being honest about wanting their opinions and preferences for course development motivates students to provide thoughtful answers. More importantly, this shows students your interest in, and respect for, their voice. If you are incorporating this technique into a credit course, use the answers to inform your syllabus. In discussing the syllabus, be clear with students about how their responses influenced the curriculum. For credit courses, revisit the DOQ responses throughout the course to reinforce that the content is mapping to students' personal goals.

Research Process Maps

One of the instructor-developed outcomes for our 100-level LIB courses is that students develop a research process. This process does not have to mirror anyone else's process. We want students to consider what they already bring to the class, what works for them, and what they learned in the class to develop their own process. We use visual mapping[9] as the technique to assess the course outcome while also providing a space for students to reflect on their own learning through the course. Angelo and Cross state that mapping is an "observable and assessable record of the students' conceptual schemata" that "allow[s] the teacher to discover the web of relationships that learners bring to the task at hand."[10] Librarians have noted that concept maps are "best used to evaluate the effectiveness of information literacy instruction focusing on concepts such as research strategy."[11] For our assessment we adopted a framework for measuring learning

9. Professor Brianne Markowski developed our department's assessment process. A full discussion of this process can be found in Brianne Markowski, "Reflecting on the Research Process: Assessing Student Learning with Pre- and Post- Concept Maps," (LOEX Annual Conference, Houston, TX, 2018).

10. Angelo and Cross, *Classroom Assessment Techniques*, 197.

11. Carolyn J. Radcliff et al., *A Practical Guide to Information Literacy Assessment for Academic Librarians* (Westport, CT: Libraries Unlimited, 2007), 107.

developed by David Hay and Ian Kinchin.[12] Students develop pre- and post-process maps on the first and last day of the course respectively. The prompts for the research process maps are:

Pre- prompt:
Think about a time when you had to research something for school. How did you start your research process? Where did you go from there?
Map out the research process you personally follow, from selecting a topic to turning in the final research project.
Post- prompt:
Take a few minutes to reflect on your research process. How has it changed based on the skills you've learned in this course? How has it stayed the same?
Map out the research process you think you will follow for future research projects, from selecting a topic to turning in the final research project.

This mapping activity serves two assessment purposes. For the librarians, it lets us see the levels of learning about the research process that take place in our eight-week course. We are not using a checklist or a rubric to assess the student research process since we know each students' process will be different and, as novice researchers, will be quite different from ours. What we seek is evidence that learning took place, as well as noting parts of the research process that are important to undergraduate students. Both can help us determine changes to our curriculum. For students, the mapping activity is a chance to reflect on their own learning and growth over the eight-week course. This provides space for them to see their learning over time that is not reflected in a course grade but in their own growth and change.

---

12. David Hay and Ian Kinchin, "Using Concept Mapping to Measure Learning Quality," *Education + Training* 50, no. 2 (2008): 167-182.

Self-Assessment

Self-assessment works to question traditional classroom dynamics by empowering students to take on the role of assessor. While self-assessment may be intimidating for students because "they have had many years of being socialized into expectations of authority-dependence and unilateral assessment by staff,"[13] this practice encourages students to think critically about their own learning and development. Self-assessment is an essential metacognitive practice that not only supports learning but also urges students to become more discerning information consumers and creators. By implementing self-assessment through a series of short, reflective activities, we work to familiarize students with the practice of self-critique, a skill that will help them both in coursework and life after college.

Research Self-Assessment

The Research Self-Assessment (RSA)[14] is implemented on the first day of a credit course or at the start of a one-shot. It helps students think about their own knowledge and skills and where they might have room for improvement. It is a time for students to reflect on themselves. It allows us to know where students feel they have the most to learn, which can help us develop assignments and the course schedule. Students answer four questions at the start of class and then discuss their answers with a peer. The RSA questions[15] are:

1. Which steps in the research process do you think you currently do well?
2. In which steps do you think you need to develop more knowledge and skill?

---

13. Boud, *Implementing Student Self-Assessment*, 13.

14. Terry Taylor et al., *100% Information Literacy Success* (Clifton Park, NY: Thomson Delmar Learning, 2007), 27.

15. These questions are adopted from Taylor et al., *100% Information Literacy Success*, 27.

3. What do you think are the most difficult steps for you to complete? Why?
4. What do you think are the easiest steps for you to complete? Why?

We have used the RSA for a pre-and post- self-assessment where students read over their responses from the first day of class and reflect on their own learning. If you are open to having students help you determine goals for a one-shot and guide the learning, the RSA is a good tool to use. When using the RSA in a one-shot, we recommend only asking questions one and two. For one-shots, use a poll to get real-time responses and engage in a conversation with students about how to spend your time. We like using Padlet[16] to get text responses that are easily batched together on the screen. Another option is a pre-survey where you ask students these questions a day or two before the one-shot session and then develop a lesson plan around the gaps students' note in the survey. In our experience, we get fewer responses with the pre-survey. However, a pre-survey does provide more time for planning and takes no time out of your one-shot session.

Research Check-In

We use a research check-in at various points in our credit courses (see **Appendix H** for prompts and student responses). These can take different forms depending on the course and the assignment. In some courses, we do a mid-course and final-course self-reflection during which students refer back to their initial check-in and discuss their progress. Here is an example of a mid- and end-of-year check-in:

Mid-Course Research Check-In:
Reflect on what you've learned so far in class and what you need to work on to improve your own research skills. Refer to the first day's self-assessment and discuss if you would answer any of these questions differently today.Discuss your own goals as a researcher.

---

16. https://padlet.com/

End-of-Year Research Check-In:

1. Reflect on what you've learned in LIB 151. Refer to the first day's self-assessment—would you answer any of these questions differently today? Discuss any changes in your research process over the last eight weeks.
2. The intended student learning outcomes for LIB 151 are:
   - Students will be able to develop a research strategy
   - Students will be able to access needed information
   - Students will be able to evaluate information
   - Students will be able to develop an argument supported by evidence

Please discuss how well you feel the course helped you to achieve these goals. Is there an outcome(s) that you feel was not met? Reflect on what you've learned in the course that is not expressed in these outcomes. Reflect on outcomes you feel are missing from this course. Reflect on your own goals as a researcher and consider how you will level-up your current skills after this class as you move into LIB 251.

Research Check-In with Goal Setting

In our 200-level course that focuses on how to write a literature review, students complete research check-ins to discuss their progress after their first draft and then again after their final draft. This reflection is combined with goal-setting as students move from draft one to draft two of their literature reviews. Examples of this check-in are below. We first ask students to answer questions; we then ask them to develop goals for their second draft and strategies for achieving those goals. Through this process, students are able to take control of their learning and their final product.

1. What do you see as the strengths in your writing?
2. Where do you see places for improvement in your writing?
3. What will you change in your second draft and why?
4. Who or what helped you most when writing your literature review? How?
5. What was the biggest hurdle you encountered when writing your literature review? How did you overcome this hurdle?
6. What are your goals for the second draft of the literature review and how will you achieve those goals?

Goal	Strategy for Achieving Goal

After the second draft of the literature review students complete another research check-in, reflecting on their goals and their process in draft two:

1. For the two questions below, refer to the goals you set in your Draft 1 self-evaluation.
    • Discuss the goals you met and reflect on how you met those goals and how they improved your second draft.
    • Discuss the goals you did not meet and reflect on why you did not meet those goals and if that affected your second draft.
2. How do you think you improved from Draft 1 to Draft 2?
3. What do you see as the strengths in your writing and has this changed since Draft 1?
4. Where do you see places for improvement in your writing? Has this changed since Draft 1?
5. What was the biggest hurdle you encountered when writing your second draft? How did you overcome this hurdle?

At the end of this 200-level course, we ask students to reflect on their own growth and areas for improvement as they move into their Honors Independent Project by answering two questions:

1. How have you grown as a writer and researcher since the first day of class?
2. Where do you still see areas for improvement in your writing and research?

If you are going to implement a research check-in, it's important to also incorporate a self-assessment at the start of class. We've found that reflection works best if students have a baseline to refer back to; they are better able to evaluate their progress if they know where they started. For one-shot instruction, the research check-in is most effective if you are embedded in a course or teaching multiple one-shots for a course. They are a great exercise to use for any course where students work on a research project throughout the semester. They are also useful for knowing where to focus your efforts in an embedded environment so that you can meet students where they are.

Group Assessment

Group assessment is a technique of self-assessment that we've found helpful when discussing topics that students find utterly boring, such as citations.[17] We used this technique for the first time in spring 2018 as a way to introduce APA citations in our credit courses. Students worked in a randomly assigned group to complete a ten-question practice quiz that covered all aspects of APA formatting and referencing. Students worked together to find the answers, engaging in discussion and peer-to-peer teaching. For us, group assessment provided a framework for planning our APA lessons for the following class sessions. Specifically, it highlighted the particular APA concepts we needed to focus on during our class discussions and activities. It also helped us assess anecdotally how our students went about finding the answers to the questions on the practice quiz. Their use of various information-seeking techniques, such as asking peers and using online resources, will help us to develop future assignments that are responsive to the existing behaviors of our students. We will continue to use group assessment and will consider other content where this approach would be beneficial.

Peer Review

Peer Review is a way that we share power in the classroom and activate student voice. We believe it is important for students to get feedback on their work from someone other than the instructor in

---

17. Group assessment is inspired by the work of Boud, *Implementing Student Self-Assessment*; and Reynolds and Trehan, "Assessment: A Critical Perspective."

order to break away from the belief that we are the only experts in the room. We also know that students come into class with varying levels of experience with research and writing; peer review allows students to share that experience with their peers.

Critical Friends Group

For students, the Critical Friends Group (CFG) is long-term peer review that happens throughout the course. The CFG is more collaborative than your typical peer review and provides space for students to build community in the classroom. We began using the CFG in the classroom in fall 2013, years before we used it in our own professional work. We first implemented it in *LIB 251: Research as Inquiry: Exploration for Beginning Researchers*,[18] and it has been a great success. Students have commented that they appreciate having someone to rely on for notes and have taken to calling a critical friend for feedback on writing outside of the course. From our perspective it is an excellent model because instructor feedback and student feedback tend to be different, so students get suggestions on their work they would not necessarily get from instructor feedback alone. What we've also observed over time is that students will always provide their peers with positive comments in peer review, so the instructor can spend more time providing feedback on areas for improvement. In the fall 2016 course, we were honest with students that we would not sandwich feedback with good-bad-good comments. Since students would get a lot of that positive feedback from their CFG, the instructor feedback would only focus on the areas that needed improvement. Students were receptive to this and appreciated our honest approach to feedback.

Setting up a CFG can be done in two ways—either an instructor can create groups or students can self-select. Either option has pros and cons. When the instructor creates groups, the students can

---

18. *LIB 251* is the second course in a four-course sequence required for students in the Upper Division Honor's Program at UNC. This course focuses on developing skills in critical reading and writing. The culmination of the course is a literature review and research proposal for the Honors Thesis project.

be grouped by major or discipline, which is helpful if students are commenting on research and writing. However, this is a top-down way to make groups and a critically-minded educator may not want to determine group make-up. If students self-select into groups, you run the risk of students grouping with their friends, and they may be less likely to be critical of group members' work. We pre-assign groups based on major/discipline and have had success. Outside of making the groups, there is no real time commitment to this model except to ensure that you provide group time in each class so that students can build relationships. We recommend groups of three to four students, but we have also seen success with groups of two. Having more than two is ideal so that students can get the perspective and experience of more than one person. One thing to watch for is dominating voices. To avoid this (as best we can), we created some activities that provide a time limit for each student giving feedback to ensure that every group member has a chance to speak.

Peer Review of Concepts/Skills

Peer review of concepts or skills that you teach in class may be one of the easier ways to incorporate peer review. We find that students are often eager to offer their peers considerate and applicable advice. We've had success using peer review for three concepts: effective research questions, choosing keywords, and writing.

Peer Review of Research Questions

Writing effective research questions can be a daunting task for students. We have found that breaking this task down into a series of drafts helps to ease the feelings of anxiety or finality that writing a research question often brings. After students develop their first draft of a research question, they do a quick self-assessment:[19]

---

19. Kate L. Turabian, Gregory G. Colomb, and Joseph M. Williams, *Student's Guide to Writing College Papers. Chicago Guides to Writing, Editing, and Publishing*, 4th ed. (Chicago: The University of Chicago Press, 2010), 38-39.

___ My research question requires research to answer.

___ My research question prompts me to develop an argument that I will support with evidence.

___ My research question can be answered with factual evidence and avoids any speculation, subjective responses, or bias.

___ My research question is focused on a specific topic or issue.

After students complete the self-assessment and make any changes, they share the question with a peer. During peer review, students offer specific suggestions for improving the research question and then revise their own research question based on the reviewer feedback.

Peer Review of Keywords

We have found that students frequently claim to feel very confident in choosing keywords for their searches. However, over the course of the research process, we have observed that these keywords often do not change, despite the need for the research to become more focused. In an effort to address this, and to tap into the expertise of our students, we have started peer review for keywords. Passing out note cards, we ask students to jot down their research topics or research questions. Then we ask for sample keywords that they have used to find their research thus far. They switch cards with a neighbor and then provide each other with suggestions for new keywords. Through this process, students are asked to think about how searches can be refined or viewed from a different perspective. This short exercise provides students with fresh ideas for their research that didn't come from their professor or a librarian. We have found that the keyword peer review is most beneficial after students have had some time to search using their original keywords.

Peer Review of Writing

There are many ways to run peer reviews of writing. In our credit courses, we ask students to go through two peer review sessions for their final assignments (these can include papers, outlines, poster presentations, lightning talks) using two techniques—Response-Centered Peer Review and Advice-Centered Peer Review.[20] In Response-Centered Peer Review, the reviewer is prompted with questions, answers those questions, and shares feedback with the writer. In Advice-Centered Peer Review, the feedback is more directive. In this peer review, the reviewer provides feedback, gives advice for improvement, and applies the assignment rubric to the writing (see **Appendix I** for student prompts).

We sometimes incorporate read-alouds into peer review, in which the author reads their own paper aloud while a reviewer listens. This allows the reviewer to hear where content is confusing, where grammatical errors are appearing, or where thoughts or arguments are not fully formed in the writing. We like this activity because it literally brings the student voice into the classroom. In addition, we encourage the utilization of student narrative through a reflection activity where we ask students to reflect on what they learned from the peer-review process, to state what changes, if any, they made based on the peer review, and to discuss why they did or did not take their peer's advice. Ideally, students realize that they can learn from healthy criticism but that, ultimately, the decisions for their writing are theirs alone.

We recommend starting any peer review with a discussion of how to give effective feedback. While students may be hesitant to criticize a peer, we find that by preempting any peer-review activity with a discussion about how to give effective and constructive feedback, we encourage students to be more thoughtful with their comments. We appreciate Boud's overview of giving and receiving feedback and have used his work in our classrooms.[21] While peer review can be a simple exchange between two students, we find that a little structure can make the process run smoother. When the parameters for the exercise are clear, students tend to

20. See the Columbia Center for Teaching and Learning document: https://ctl.columbia.edu/files/2017/10/2017.10.11.teacherslounge-flavorsofpeerreview-27a3d7h.pdf.

21. Boud, *Implementing Student Self-Assessment*.

proceed with more confidence. Whether you are incorporating Advice-Centered or Response-Centered Peer Review, we suggest having pre-determined questions that guide the reviewer and the peer discussion. We also suggest setting time limits that ensure there is enough time for significant feedback. For example, given ten minutes to discuss a paper with a peer would produce some criticism, while thirty minutes would most likely result in a much deeper, richer dialogue between peers. We also recommend doing some space planning. It can be chaotic and unproductive having twenty or more students in a classroom reading to each other. Planning for partners to find quiet places outside the classroom will make this activity much more manageable for all involved.

Involving Students in Assessment Practice

In this section we discuss two ways we have involved students in the assessment and curriculum process through Collaborative Development of Student Learning Outcomes and Collaborative Rubric Design. Through these two activities, we work toward sharing power with our students, creating a space for true dialogue and centering student voice in the classroom.

Collaborative Student Learning Outcome Development

Collaborating with students to develop learning outcomes is another technique that we implement in our credit courses.[22] On the first day of the semester, just after giving an overview of the course, we invite students to think about and articulate their learning goals for the class through a think-pair-share activity. First, they reflect on their personal learning goals, then partner up with a peer to share their goals. After discussion in pairs, students form groups of four or five. Within these larger groups, students combine personal learning goals to develop a short list of shared learning goals. Each group develops anywhere between three to six goals. The groups

---

37. This can be adopted for one-shot instruction by using the Personal Learning Goals Activity discussed earlier in this chapter.

then share their goals in a class discussion and engage with each other to finalize learning outcomes for the course.

The first time we implemented this was in spring 2018. During the conversation, we let the students determine their own learning outcomes but did not provide any information about the course outcomes important to us. After the learning outcomes were compiled, they were added to the official syllabus for the class. The collaboratively developed student learning outcomes were listed alongside our own student learning outcomes for the class, illustrating their equal importance. We made changes to the course schedule based on the new learning outcomes to ensure that the students' goals were reflected in the course. During the next class period we discussed with the students how their feedback was incorporated into the syllabus and course schedule. We even mapped their learning outcomes to our learning outcomes to show how similar they were.

Unfortunately, we feel we missed the mark on our first attempt at student-developed outcomes. We realized that, during the process of developing the outcomes, we gave away our authority for fear of being authoritarian. We missed the collaborative nature of outcome development by not bringing our own outcomes into the discussion. We presented two equal lists of outcomes on the syllabus, but we should have negotiated a single list of outcomes, combining them to integrate both student and instructor needs. Of course, everything is a learning process. We will continue to involve students in developing course outcomes but will work on making the process truly collaborative.

Collaborative Rubric Design[23]

In Collaborative Rubric Design (CRD), students co-create the rubric that is used to score their assignments. We've implemented this in a credit course where students co-created the rubric for a

---

23. For a detailed description of our experience with Collaborative Rubric Design, see Dineen and McCartin, "An Unfinished Journey."

literature review assignment. We collectively developed a rubric for the paper's first draft, then we worked together to revise the rubric for the final draft. Students worked in pairs to determine the paper components they wanted scored (e.g., Conclusion) and then determined rankings (e.g., Good, Needs Improvement) and points associated with each ranking. Thus, students decided which parts of the assignment would be graded and how much the assignment would be worth toward their final grade. In some areas the students were harsher than we would have been! Students were receptive to CRD, noting, "I believe that being included in the course design as a student is essential in making a good class." Another student commented: "I really appreciated being involved in course development through the rubric development process... I felt more motivated in this course than any other course."

Our first implementation of CRD was a learning experience. We were so determined to involve students in curriculum design that we actually excluded ourselves from the process of designing the rubric. Students created a ranking category titled "You Suck," and we let that stand. We thought telling the students they could not do something in their own rubric defeated the purpose of the activity. Upon reflection, we realized that by not speaking up, Collaborative Rubric Design was not collaborative at all. Just as in the student learning outcome development, we were too concerned with sharing power with our students, and the result was that we gave up power completely. Our desire to reject authoritarianism pushed us to reject our own authority, which Freire warned against.[24] Creating a community in the classroom means that everyone gets a say and has equal voice in the conversation. The most important thing to remember when you involve students in practice, whether in a credit course or a one-shot, is that you are an authority in the classroom, and that you need to bring your expertise into the conversation.

---

24. Beatty, "Reading Freire for First-World Librarians," 6

Wrap-Up

Throughout this chapter, we have focused on classroom assessment strategies that follow the tenets of the CIPF. By taking a critically-minded approach to assessment, we nurture more inclusive and democratic learning environments for our students. We shared two experiences about failing to share power with students to illustrate that critical practice is a learning process. We've discussed authority versus authoritarianism multiple times in this book, because it is one of the biggest lessons we've learned over the past two years working together. We hope this chapter has provided some new ideas for your own assessment practice. We continue to experiment with and improve upon this work. If you implement any of these techniques, please share your experiences with us and talk to us about improvements you've made! In the next chapter, we will delve into what we anticipate for the future of our critical-inclusive assessment practice.

Chapter 5

TOWARD A (MORE) CRITICAL-INCLUSIVE ASSESSMENT PRACTICE

Assessment has been "criticized as a form of neoliberal accountability," and as a "form of control."[1] We disagree that critical information literacy and assessment are fundamentally incompatible. We are convinced, and hope that we've shown throughout this book, that assessment has a place in our pedagogical practices and does not have to hinder our attempts to uphold critical, feminist, or inclusive ideals. Assessment and a critical-inclusive pedagogy can work together in practice. We applaud the courage of Anne Jumonville Graf and Benjamin Harris when they claim that "critical pedagogy can actually be facilitated through assessment practices."[2] We support their argument that "assessment methods, as well as our beliefs about the purpose and design of assessment... help create the space where critical pedagogy can flourish rather than limit its potential."[3] As educators, it's our responsibility to know if students are learning and to reflect on our own teaching.

---

1. Lua Gregory and Shana Higgins, "Reorienting an Information Literacy Program Toward Social Justice: Mapping the Core Values of Librarianship to the ACRL Framework," *Communications in Information Literacy* 11, no. 1 (2017): 47.

2. Harris and Jumonville, "Assessment is Dead, Long Live Assessment," presentation script shared with authors in personal communication.

3. Harris and Jumonville, "Assessment is Dead, Long Live Assessment," presentation script shared with authors in personal communication.

Ultimately, it is our responsibility as educators to understand if and how learning is happening, and if it isn't, it's our responsibility to improve the learning environment. To ignore assessment is irresponsible.

We continue to use the CIPF as a guide for our work. It pushes us to prioritize teaching and assessment strategies that make students co-creators in the teaching-learning process. The CIPF helps us to center students in our practice and helps students gain the confidence to challenge ideas. As we've said, it is unlikely that students will achieve critical consciousness through information literacy one-shot instruction or even credit courses. We aren't assessing "changed lives,"[4] but by using the CIPF as a holistic foundation, we can work to foster critical consciousness through our pedagogical practice.

We recognize that we still have work to do on our journey toward critical practice. We will work to bring conversations of oppression into our one-shots and credit courses. Our goal is to design short-term special topics courses around critical issues such as information privilege. In such courses we would delve into deeper discussions with students about power and control in information, costs, access, and the still present digital divide. We also need to work on attending to the affective components of learning, and on developing more critical-inclusive assessments. The affective components of learning are essential to implementing a critical-inclusive practice. This is what bell hooks referred to as "a union of mind, body, and spirit,"[5] stressing the importance of attending to the whole student. But how is this done effectively in practice, especially in typical one-shot instruction? This requires more reading and critical reflection on our part. We plan to bring all of these discussions to our department as part of our bi-monthly

---

4. Eamon Tewell, "The Practice and Promise of Critical Information Literacy: Academic Librarians' Involvement in Critical Information Literacy," *College & Research Libraries* 79, no. 1 (2018): 23.

5. bell hooks discusses the work of Paulo Freire and the Buddhist monk Thich Nhat Hanh, both of whom had a profound impact on her teaching. She notes that Freire was more interested in the mind, while Thich Nhat Hanh took a more holistic approach to learning. hooks, *Teaching to Transgress*, 14.

theory meetings as a new avenue for exploration. Finally, we will also continue to refine our critical-inclusive assessment practice by experimenting with new assessments, which is the focus of this chapter.

Future Assessment

There are additional assessments we would like to incorporate into our teaching, including using focus groups with our credit courses, implementing Course Reflection Groups, expanding collaborative rubric design, working with student portfolios, and incorporating more reflection.

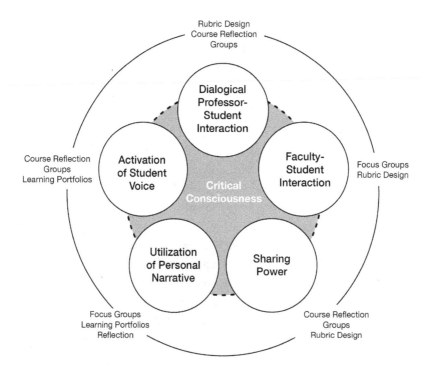

Figure 9: Future Assessment Mapped to the CIPF

Course Reflection Groups

Course Reflection Groups is a technique that we are particularly excited about implementing. We will invite students to provide contemporaneous feedback about class content, grading practices, and teaching styles in small group meetings. The intent of these meetings is to engage in dialogue with our students during the semester, rather than after. The feedback gathered will result in real time curricular changes. Shor discusses a similar practice through his "after-class group" in which he and a group of students would, after each class, evaluate and make changes to future lesson plans.[6] He would speak only sparingly in these meetings, and ask simple questions of his students, such as *how did class go?* and *what did you like/dislike about class today?*[7] We want to take a similar approach. Our goal is to provide a forum for our students to discuss what is supporting or detracting from their learning goals. This practice of continually checking in is an essential part of sharing power with our students.

Focus Groups

In an effort to garner more meaningful feedback from our students we want to use focus groups with our credit courses. At the end of each semester we will invite a small group of students from different sections and different courses to discuss specific issues with the curriculum. We want students to share their opinions about the course content as well as their experience as students in the course. We'll ask students to reflect on their experiences with assignments and reflect critically on their role in the course. We will then use this feedback to inform our lesson plans for the next semester. We believe that this type of engaged assessment can help build positive relationships with our students. Furthermore, we

6. Shor, *Empowering Education*, 161.

7. Shor, *Empowering Education*, 162.

believe that by using these focus groups to ask students to reflect on their time in our classes, we are centering student experience and working toward a more democratic classroom.

Learning Portfolios

The learning portfolio is an assessment technique that is frequently discussed in the literature of critical and feminist pedagogies. We see portfolio assessments that encompass student-chosen work and self-reflection as the embodiment of student narrative. Our curiosity in delving into this type of assessment has led us to think that portfolios are a great way to strengthen departmental relationships in our liaison areas. For instance, art and design students are accustomed to producing portfolios of their work between their first and second years in the program. By working with our departmental faculty, we could incorporate or strengthen information literacy concepts into existing portfolio criteria. Portfolios can also help facilitate collaboration between librarians and disciplinary faculty. If we work with students and faculty to develop portfolios over a four-year degree program it will give us insight into how student information literacy is developing, where there are gaps in student skills and understanding, and where additional instruction is warranted. We plan to seek grant funding through our university's assessment office in 2019 to start a collaborative portfolio project with disciplinary faculty.

Reflection

Learning journals are another way to assess the progression of student learning over time and to highlight student voice through personal reflection. Currently, we ask our students to do a series of reflective writing activities that are disconnected from each other. Starting in fall 2018, we plan to implement learning journals that will have students reflecting from the first to the last day on their research skills, as well as on more critical concepts such as their beliefs about access and costs and their own growth as researchers.[8] For more reflection on our teaching, we have discussed using video recordings as a way to assess and reflect on our teaching methods. This will be a continuation of our library-wide peer observation project. We are interested in exploring this type of assessment because it will incorporate the knowledge of our peers with our own reflections drawn from watching ourselves in action.

Rubric Design

We've explored rubric development done during class, which is a helpful exercise for students and brings their voices into the classroom. But there is less time for significant student-teacher dialogue when rubric development takes place during class time. Our next project is to work with students in a credit course to develop a rubric for the final project, an annotated outline. We would like to invite five students to join us in analyzing and assessing this final assignment during a four-hour workshop. During this workshop, we hope to create a rubric for the next semester that is both well thought out and understandable for students. Through this project, we hope to gain insight into students' perceptions of the assessment process, to encourage students to take authorship in the assessment of their work, and to co-create an assessment process that includes their voices. Our ultimate goal is that every rubric we use in one-shots or credit courses is designed collaboratively with students.

---

8. A good overview of using research journals in the library classroom can be found in Louse R. Fluk, "Foregrounding the Research Log in Information Literacy Instruction," *Journal of Academic Librarianship* 41, (2015) 488-498. For a more recent discussion about using learning journals during a course, see Kari Weaver and Michelle Petrie, "Sociology in Action: A Comparative Study of Embedded Interventions for Improved Research and Writing in the Introduction of Sociological Research Method" (Presentation at Librarians Information Literacy Conference, April 2018).

Final Thoughts

At the 2018 Librarian's Information Literacy Annual Conference, Kyle Feenstra posed the following question: "How can the library make space for the voice of the learner, ensuring that it is visible and validated as a meaningful expression alongside the privileged voices of academics and dominant university discourses?"[9] We hope that we've presented part of the answer to this question. Although we will never know if our practice of sharing power with them, involving them, hearing them, and caring about them will help our students break down systemic power structures, we do know that our practice makes a space for them in our library and in our classroom. We will continue to foster democratic classrooms that center students and their experience. We will move our work forward, build on it, learn from our mistakes, and continue to learn from our students.

9. Kyle Feenstra, "The Process is the Outcome: A Framework for Student 'Research as Praxis,'" (Presented at Librarians' Information Literacy Annual Conference, Liverpool, UK, April 2018).

Appendix A: Peer Observation of Teaching Process & Forms

Peer observation for University Libraries Credit Courses is an activity of the Curriculum Committee, used to improve teaching and learning; it is non-evaluative. No documentation from the peer observation will appear in annual or comprehensive faculty dossiers.

Pre-Meeting

The pre-meeting will be called by the observed instructor. The observed instructor will discuss the lesson plan and objectives for the class being observed. The observed instructor will determine what the observer should focus on during the class. The focus of the peer observation is the choice of the observed instructor.

During the pre-meeting, the observed instructor will fill out page one of the Peer Class Observation Form.

Observation

During the observation, the observer will sit in the back of the classroom. The observer will focus on what the observed instructor wants the observer to pay attention to during the session. The observer may take hand-written notes during the observation. No electronic devices should be used for note-taking.

After the session, the observer will fill out page two of the Peer Class Observation Form.

Post-Meeting

The post-meeting will be called by the observed instructor within one week of the observation. This meeting will focus specifically on the previously determined focus areas. During the post-meeting, the observed instructor will discuss his or her perceptions of the session. Subsequently, the observer will describe his or her perceptions of the session. The observer will provide the observed instructor with typed notes on the Peer Class Observation Form.

Verbal Course Feedback

On the final day of class, the observed instructor will provide 15-20 minutes at the end of class for verbal course feedback from students. This will be led by the observer and the observed instructor will leave the classroom. The observed instructor will 1) provide the observer with questions to ask the students, and 2) be responsible for scheduling the observer or finding a replacement when necessary. The observer will 1) take notes during the verbal feedback session and 2) deliver the notes from the session to the observed instructor. The observed will only take notes on content of the discussion and no identifying factors of the students will be recorded.

Peer Observation Form
University Libraries' Curriculum Committee

Confidentiality considerations: *The purpose of the Peer Class Observation is to maintain our goal of teaching excellence within the University Libraries' credit course program and to provide a venue for us to share teaching ideas and strategies with each other. In order for the Peer Class Observation to be effective, it is crucial that we establish and maintain an environment of mutual respect and trust. Therefore, all critiques given on this form should be done in a constructive manner, and the raw data gathered through our observations in each other's classes and recorded on this form is to be kept confidential. All copies of the completed peer class observation form should be given to the observed faculty member. All faculty members are encouraged to share particularly effective teaching strategies with colleagues, and also to share any difficulties so that we can all be engaged in cooperative problem solving. Under no circumstances should copies of completed Class Observation Forms be included in Evaluation and Promotion/Tenure dossiers.*

Observer: _____

Class Observed: _____
Date and Time of Class: _____

To be completed by the faculty member being observed:
1) The goals or outcomes I have in mind for my students during this class session are:

2) During this class session, I would like the observer to pay particular attention to, and give me feedback on the following:

To be completed by the observer:
1) Describe what happened in this class session. What was done by the faculty member and/or the students? What teaching methods

did you observe? How effective were these activities and methods in achieving the goal or student outcome that the faculty member had set out for this class session? Explain.

2) What "worked" particularly well during this class session? Were there any small-group activities, assignments, or teaching strategies that you think the faculty member should share with other faculty members?

3) Was there a point during this class session when the faculty member "lost" student attention? How did the faculty member react? How did the faculty member regain student attention?

4) What suggestions do you have for the faculty member you observed in terms of expansion of particularly effective teaching strategies, improvement of teaching strategies that didn't work well, solving problems you observed, etc.?

5) Other comments or observations

Appendix B: Peer Observation Checklist

Developed by Piper Martin, Assistant Professor, University of Illinois, Urbana-Champaign

These two lists can provide ideas about what the instructor/ observee would like the observer to focus on during the peer review session. The checklists will not be used to evaluate the instructor.

List adapted from:
Brewerton, A. (2004). How I joined the Triads: The launch of a peer observation and review scheme at Oxford Brookes University Library. *SCONUL Newsletter, 31*, 35-44.

Introduction
- Were the objectives of the session made clear?
- Were anticipated learning outcomes identified?
- Did the session begin on time?
- Was the structure of the lesson clear?

Planning and Organization
- Was the session related to previous sessions/related to the rest of the course?
- Was the structure set out at the start?
- Did the session appear to be well-planned and well-organized?

Methods/Approach
- Were the methods/approach taken suitable to achieve the learning objectives?
- What alternative approaches could have been taken?

Delivery and Pace
- Did the pace and delivery seem appropriate for the students present?

- Were there any aspects, in your opinion, dealt with too briefly/in too much detail?
- Did the session seem rushed/drawn out?

Content
- Where you feel qualified to comment, did the content seem accurate and up-to-date?
- Were appropriate examples given?
- Was the session pitched at the appropriate level for those students present?
- Did the content match the students' needs?

Student Participation
- Were students invited to participate?
- How was this managed?
- Did it seem planned?
- Did participation enable the instructor to check the students' understanding?

Learning Resources
- Were any kind of learning objects or tools used?
- If so, were they clear and well-produced?
- Were handouts used?
- If so, were they well-produced and relevant to the lesson?
- Did the resources contribute to or detract from the session?

Accommodation
- Was the room/accommodation suitable for the session?
- Was seating arrangement appropriate?

Overall Style and Ambiance
- Did the instructor appear confident in delivery?
- Did they convey enthusiasm?
- Were they clear and audible?
- Was there good rapport with the students?

- Was the instructor in tune with the students?

Feedback
- Was student feedback solicited?
- How does feedback relate to the comments above?

IS Instruction & Training Checklist for Observations

From:
Middleton, C. (2002). "Evolution of peer evaluation of library instruction at Oregon State University Libraries." *portal: Libraries and the Academy*, 2(1), 69-78.

Presentation Skills
- Has adequate vocal delivery (audible, varied, interesting, clear and distinct)
- Demonstrates interest in and enthusiasm for the subject matter
- Uses effective/appropriate body movement (gestures, avoids standing in one spot)
- Uses visuals and/or technology appropriately (can be seen; contributes to class
- understanding)
- Makes eye contact with participants

Clarity of Presentation
- Avoids jargon
- Explains terms and concepts
- Uses examples to illustrate concepts
- Summarizes main points
- Organized/sticks to the point
- Avoids irrelevant details
- Avoids unnecessary repetition

Content
- The purpose of the class/workshop was clearly stated

- The material covered was appropriate (neither too elementary nor too complex)
- The level of instruction was appropriate (neither too elementary nor too complex)
- The amount of information was appropriate
- The pace of the session was appropriate
- There was enough time for hands-on practice (if applicable)
- There was enough time for questions and/or discussion

Relationship with Participants/Students
- Shows understanding of participants needs
- Encourages and responds to questions
- Students seem interested
- Encourages and provides opportunities for active participation
- Is approachable/helpful
- Identified sources of further help (consulting desks, office hours)
- Is aware of participants (notices confusion, distractions, hands-raised, etc.)

Relationship with Classroom Instructor (if appropriate)
- Has adequate knowledge/understanding of course assignment
- Involves instructor during the class

Appendix C: Peer Observation Notes

Peer Review of Teaching Form

UNC-UW Inter-Institutional Peer Observation Collaboration

Confidentiality considerations: *The purpose of this peer review of teaching pilot program is to maintain the goal of teaching excellence at each institution by participating in this pilot program. We hope the program will give us new perspectives and provide a venue for us to share teaching ideas and strategies with each other. In order for this program to be effective, it is crucial that we establish and maintain an environment of mutual respect and trust. Therefore, all critiques given on this form should be done in a constructive manner, and the raw data gathered through our observations in each other's classes and recorded on this form is to be kept confidential. All copies of the completed peer class observation form should be given to the observed faculty member. All faculty members are encouraged to share particularly effective teaching strategies with the participants of this pilot program and also to share any difficulties so that we can all be engaged in cooperative problem solving. Under no circumstances should copies of completed Class Observation Forms be included in Evaluation and Promotion/Tenure dossiers.*

Observer: Deleted for Confidentiality

Class Observed: LIB 151 (Evaluating Sources)

Class Composition (i.e., majors, non-majors, etc.): honors students

Date and Time of Class: Thursday 9:30-10:45 am (1/19/2017)

To be completed by the faculty member being observed:

1) The goals or outcomes I have in mind for my students during this class session are:

- Identifying primary and secondary sources (e.g., research studies vs non-research studies)
- Identifying the differences between primary research and literature reviews
- Identifying scholarly and popular sources
- Determining Relevance of a source to a topic

2) During this class session I would like the observer to pay particular attention to and give me feedback on the following:
- My ability to convey information clearly
- My ability to run the multiple class activities in terms of moving easily from one to the next
- Connection between the activities and content

To be completed by the observer:

1) Describe what happened in this class session. What was done by the faculty member and/or the students? What teaching methods did you observe? How effective were these activities and methods in achieving the goal or student outcome that the faculty member had set out for this class session? Explain.

This was a lively, activity-packed, very well-run class session. Students did all the work in a pair and a group of three, so even when they began an activity working individually, they consulted with their group members before discussing their results as a class. The faculty member mainly served as a discussion facilitator when she spoke with each group, clarifying terms and concepts, and helping the students to tease out answers to their own questions. She also used a PowerPoint presentation to shape the agenda of the class and to define terminology; at no point did she read from the slides or lecture the class. Rather, she used the presentation as a springboard from which to give examples and flesh out the ideas/concepts that were the focus of the class.

The teaching methods were active, student-centered learning. There were four varied activities that either reinforced new information that the instructor presented or that the students had read about outside of class. The activities connected clearly to the goals the instructor set for the session; for example, the first activity connected to a chart of social science research that the students had already received/reviewed, to the kind of research papers that the students themselves would be doing both at the end of this semester and the next, and to the homework reading that the students had done prior to coming to class. A discussion followed each of the activities during which students had a chance to ask questions or to unpack some of the concepts or terminology. The instructor did a good job judging when the groups were done talking before bringing the class together for a larger discussion.

2) What are the particular aspects of the session being observed? What worked particularly well during this class session in regards to the specific aspects of the class session that the instructor asked about?

Instructor's ability to convey information clearly.

The faculty member did this extremely well. There was a judicious amount of information on the slides and she did an excellent job explaining the various concepts and terms associated with the class topics. She had several great examples, such as the difference between scholarly and professional literature in response to a student's question (a criminal justice scholar works with criminal justice topics but is not a criminal justice practitioner walking a beat) and she drew good distinctions, such as how to appropriately use tertiary or secondary sources to inform one's reading of primary sources, and the difference between opinions and the conclusions of primary research studies. She answered student questions thoroughly and definitely understood what they were asking. She also was good at facilitating the class discussion, allowing the students to talk it out without jumping in and correcting them.

Instructor's ability to run the multiple class activities in terms of moving easily from one to the next.

Overall, the transitions between the activities went very smoothly. There was progressive movement throughout the presentation (or review) of information, time for questions, the activity reinforced the information so the students could put the concept into action, group discussion, class discussion and clarification, then moving on to the next concept/topic. The order in which she presented the four main concepts/topics flowed nicely as well.

Connection between the activities and content.

The faculty member did a stellar job making this explicit. Throughout the class session, she referred to the goals of the major assignment this semester and connected them to the day's topics and activities; how the content and/or knowledge they were learning today would affect their understanding of their major assignment next semester; how the previous class session's information interweaves with today's class session information; and how their homework relates to both the class session today as well as the next class session. This, I believe, is particularly important, because students often view information literacy instruction as "busy work," or they don't see how it hooks into other assignments or other classes—even though this is a class that is specifically connected to their honors program, it's crucial for librarians to emphasize the universal nature of IL, and she did that admirably well.

Beyond the big picture, the activities all meshed beautifully with the content of what was being presented; for example, after learning about the differences among scholarly, trade, and popular publications and what each might offer the researcher, the activity was to rank the source value of different sources depending on the topic that each group was given. So the students had an opportunity to once again decide what kind of source was on each card (reinforcing the information and the previous activity) and then figure out how relevant/useful the sources were in relation to each other within the context of the given topic (stretch practice of new information). Bravo!

3) How did the instructor engage with the students?

She was very relaxed and it was obvious to me that she had a good rapport with the students: greeting them as they arrived in the classroom, chatting easily with them before class started, and interacting fluidly as they engaged in group discussion and in the class discussion. She used humor effectively and she managed to be both approachable and authoritative. Of course, the well-planned class and thoughtful activities also engaged the students as well!

4) What suggestions do you have for the faculty member you observed in terms of expansion of particularly effective teaching strategies, improvement of teaching strategies that didn't work well, solving problems you observed, etc.?

I saw very little—and certainly nothing major—to criticize or suggest improvements upon.

- There was no agenda or overview for that day's session. This is probably less important in a credit class that meets twice a week than in a one-shot or a once a week class, but I think it still has the advantage of giving the students an idea of the structure and movement of the day's activities and content. It might also have helped with the next bullet point.
- The only disjointed transition between one activity and the next was moving between the very first thing the students did in class (a short discussion of their potential topics for the paper

in the class) and the main content of the day's session. Perhaps as a transition the instructor could have said something like "As you refine your topic idea, remember that for this class, you'll be conducting a secondary study. Let's dig into identifying the differences between primary and secondary research."

- The slide about what search terms they might use in Summon to locate certain types of articles seemed random and not really connected to anything else. I think it can be removed and added later in the course, or be added to a session with a search strategy activity (e.g., you can use the name/kind of a study to find articles using that method).

- The discussion of non-experts, and why journalists are examples of non-experts, didn't resolve well. This was probably due to the fact that time was running out at the point where it came up, but I was not convinced that the students were satisfied with the answer that journalists are not experts.

5) Other comments or observations:

The class was a joy to observe! The faculty member is an organized, engaging teacher.

Appendix D: Face-to-Face Feedback Data

What about this class did you find most beneficial to you as a student/researcher?

- Everything APA, but especially the in-text citations.
- The Excel template was really helpful to organize my research; I will use this again for research papers.
- It was great that all the due dates were spread out and everything wasn't just due at the end.
- I really like how the annotated outline, the introduction, and the lit review were all separate assignments. It made it more manageable and way less overwhelming.
- RefWorks was great. I knew that we could use it, but learning how to use it was super helpful.
- All the new databases and resources we learned about were really great.

Is there any part of this class that you felt was extraneous or irrelevant?

- This may not be what you're looking for, but I feel that the quizzes are weighted too much. I did really well on everything else, but I didn't do well on the quizzes and it really hurt my grade.
- I'd like to spend more time on APA and less time on primary/ secondary sources. APA is more important.

If you could change anything about this class for future LIB 160 students, what would it be?

- More time on writing the paper.
- I'd never written a lit review before and more time on how to write APA style lit reviews would be helpful.
- More defined expectations on the lit review, and more separated into chunks.

- (from a different student than before) The quizzes were given too much weight. It hurt my grade, too.
- (in response from another student) I don't think the quizzes need to change. They were open note, take home, and Professor Dineen told us to take good notes.
- (from another student) Maybe Professor Dineen could give 3 quizzes—one early, one middle, and one at the end—that would help; or, if she allowed one redo on a quiz; or maybe not have quizzes at all.

Think back to the first day of class. Do you feel like the answers you gave in the Day One Questionnaire were reflected in the structure of the class?
(multiple comments from students that they had no idea what they wrote on the Day One Questionnaire, that it was too long ago; so I asked the students what they thought of the overall structure of the class)
- I really liked how Professor Dineen laid everything out, told us why we were doing it, and that she graded so quickly. I am in my third year at UNC and she is the most organized professor I've had and it was really helpful to have the purpose/criteria on everything explained.
- It would be really nice to have another in-class day to write the paper and be able to ask questions while I'm writing.
- I didn't really like the way we chose topics; I didn't like any of the topics I got to choose from. It'd be better if we could just pick any topic we like related to criminal justice.

Think back to your assignments like Identifying Literature Types and the Summary Table. You all decided as a group that you preferred to earn completion/effort grades. Do you feel like that type of grading was helpful to your learning? Why or why not?
- Yes, very helpful. We got to improve, without it being punitive.
- I liked the effort grades for the first seven weeks of class; it kept you honest no matter what because if you didn't make an effort, it would show in the final paper.

- No matter what, even with the effort grades, you were still learning. It just wasn't as stressful, but I still had to figure it out. I couldn't just skate by, like I thought I'd be able to do.
- Anything else?
- The syllabus was really detailed and we knew what was expected, but Professor Dineen was still really flexible, which was great.
- She was constantly checking in with, making sure we understood stuff, and were ready to move on to the next thing.

Appendix E: Focus Group Interview Questions

Instructor Interview Questions
1. Tell us your name and your favorite book/T.V. show.
2. What role or purpose does the library session have for your ENG 122 class?
3. What do you find most helpful about library session?
4. What do you find least helpful about library session?
5. Role of library session in helping achieve overall course goals. On the paper in front of you, write your goals for your students. Then hand out the library session learning goals. Write how the library goals align with your goals for the course. COLLECT AT END OF FOCUS GROUP.
   a) Share your thoughts on how the library goals align with your goals for the course.
   b) How could the library session be improved so that it better helps you achieve your goals for the course?
6. What assignments do you use in ENG 122 that require students to search for and get outside sources like journal articles or books?
7. How does the library session help your students complete their class assignments?
8. If you were in charge of the library session, what changes would you make to improve it?
9. Is there anything you would like to add about the library session, or anything we missed?

Student Interview Questions
1. Tell us who you are; what your major is (or possible major if still deciding) and what your favorite book/T.V. show is?
2. Think back to a research paper or project you completed prior to coming to UNC (high school, community college, etc.).

How did you find books, magazines, and other information for that paper or project?

3. We are interested in knowing what you think the purpose is of the library session for your ENG 122 class. Why do you think your ENG 122 instructor had your class attend the library session?

4. Role of library session in helping with assignments. Students given a chart with activities related to what is taught in the ENG 122 library session. COLLECT AT END OF FOCUS GROUP. Follow up: What activities have you done? What assignments have you done that require you to search for and get outside sources like journal articles or books? How did the library session help you complete those assignments?

5. What did you find most helpful about library session?

6. What did you find least helpful about library session?

7. What else do you think you still need to know about library research to succeed on your assignments?

8. If you were in charge of the library session, what changes would you make to improve the session?

9. Is there anything you would like to add about the library session, or anything we missed?

Appendix F: Mapping Personal Learning Goals to Course Outcome

Course Goal	Student Personal Learning Goals
Develop a research process.	Pre-planning the paper/time use
	I would like to learn the fastest and most efficient ways to research topics
	Being able to research, compile and write a paper quickly.
	Be more time efficient and detailed in my research
	finding reliable sources in a more timely manner
	Organizing Evidence
	Learn how to organize evidence and research
	I would like to improve my organizational skills in terms of information gathered from sources.
	efficiency in writing longer papers with ways to outline better.
	Better organize my data that I collected for my paper.
	organizing the writing/outline
	get better at organizing the evidence found from my sources
	becoming better at organizing evidence from a paper
	Organizing ideas better.
	Organization
	Organizing the information I pull from sources and how to keep them so that I don't struggle finding the pieces I'll need to fit into my paper.

Course Goal	Student Personal Learning Goals
Demonstrate effective search strategies.	Research from books and essays online Being able to navigate sources easier and more efficient. Learn how to find evidence in not just online sources Expanding my search more than Google can help Find better ways to find topic research Learn how to find my research information in an easier manner
Evaluate information.	Finding reliable sources in a more timely manner I want to be able to find qualified credible sources finding good quality articles Understanding the difference between good and bad sources to use for a paper as well as what sources are appropriate in utilizing for a research project. Finding sources that are relevant and useful to my paper. Finding sources that apply to my topic Credible evidence Finding sources that are credible finding the most accurate information and evidence for a paper How to tell if the information found is sufficient easier ways to find credible information to use in my papers. Skills in finding the best sources for the paper the first time

Course Goal	Student Personal Learning Goals
Develop an argument supported by evidence.	APA Formatting and Citations (29 comments)
	Consistency in writing research papers so that it becomes second nature
	being able to write a paper that is scholarly.
	Cohesive paragraphs just relating to one topic
	I would like to be able to determine how much research is too much research. For example, how to I condense the information and apply to my project while still keeping it at an appropriate amount.
	Better my writing skills
	Creating one solid theme for the whole paper
	Creating and maintaining a strong thesis statement without necessarily deviating from it throughout the course of the project.
	be confident in my writing
	Working sources into my papers more smoothly
	Concepts of how much or how little quoting is appropriate
	I want to be able not struggle so much while trying to narrow my research topic.
	Placing my researched sources throughout my essay
	Explanations of sources
	Make paper flow well

Appendix G: Day One Questionnaire

1) What do you hope to take away from this course? Please rank your answers from what you are most interested in discussing, to what you are least interested in discussing.
- Ways to use library and information resources more efficiently
- Strategies for tackling research projects
- Strategies for being a more thoughtful information consumer and creator
- Knowledge of APA formatting and citation standards
- Greater understanding of information sources in the Social Sciences
- Strategies for evaluating multiple types of information
- Other?

2) When it comes to research for a writing assignment, when do you feel most confident? Please rank your answers from most confident to least confident.
- Writing a research question
- Finding relevant sources
- Evaluating information sources
- Citing your sources
- Formatting the paper
- Writing and editing the paper
- Other?

3) In what ways do you feel like you learn best? Please choose all answers that apply.
- Listening to lectures and taking notes
- Discussing concepts with a partner
- Class conversations
- In-class activities
- Preparing for and taking quizzes/exams
- Reflective writing
- Reading assigned texts
- Watching assigned videos

4) **In what ways do you prefer to receive feedback?** Please rank
your answers from most preferred to least preferred.
- Face-to-face discussions
- Written feedback
- Number/letter grades

Appendix H: Research Check-In Student Responses

Mid-Class Check-In

Reflect on what you've learned so far in class and what you need to work on to improve your own research skills. Refer to the first day's self-assessment and discuss if you would answer any of these questions differently today. Discuss your own goals as a researcher.

The research process tends to be a little different for everyone. Although my first step in the research process tends to be to panic, I've found that the steps lined out so far in this class help to simplify and organize the research process. Understanding how to use keywords when trying to find a book in Summon and Encore was especially helpful for me. Gaining a working knowledge of how these resources work has helped me to better search for and find the tools I need. However, the most helpful part of this class for me has been understanding how to read and analyze a primary source. By breaking down the piece into Intro, Abstract, etc., it made looking at a daunting article so much more manageable.

I do not think that I would probably answer any of the questions from the first day differently, but I know that now I have a better understanding of how to approach the project in general and would be able to be much more efficient in finding and sifting through sources, which makes the entire process a whole lot less painful than it normally is for me.

To improve I think that I will be able to benefit most when we talk about how to organize and cite sources within the paper you are writing. For me, that is the hardest part of the process. I would like to be able to better organize my writing so that it flowed well and that citations were done properly. Currently, I tend to "over-cite" information because I'm not sure how much I'm "allowed" to talk in the paper, and I get nervous about putting too much of my personal opinion in the paper. I would like to figure out how to balance and synthesize these two things—personal opinion and researched information.

Check-In with Goal Setting

1. What do you see as the strengths in your writing?

I think I've done a good job of making clear points and tying back all of my sources to those points. I've taken a strong stance on the literature and I back it up. I put a lot of passion into my writing and that is important to me.

2. Where do you see places for improvement in your writing?

My organization gets a little messy at times and I think the order I put things in doesn't always make sense. My passion in writing can come off as a little tangenty at times so, I need to fix that. I sometimes make assumptions that people have the same knowledge I do, and I think I can make certain points clearer by just giving a little more background information.

3. What will you change in your second draft and why?

The organization of the draft will change. I'm putting the sections in a different order that makes more sense. I'm specifying places that were unclear to my professor, my advisor and my critical friends group. I'm generally fixing grammar and things that didn't read clearly to others.

4. Who or what helped you most when writing your literature review? How?

Writing the first draft, I felt like just having all of my sources and being able to plug them into my points was super helpful, but the best thing was the criticism I received after my first draft from my professor, critical friends group and advisor. It made things so much more clear and showed me exactly what I needed to do to continue.

5. What was the biggest hurdle you encountered when writing your literature review? How did you overcome this hurdle?

Probably organization. I don't know why it was so hard to figure out where to put things, but it really was extremely complicated.

6. What are your goals for the second draft of the literature review and how will you achieve those goals?

Goal	Strategy for Achieving Goal
Reorganization	Switching sections to make more sense
Specificity	Identifying the points that were unclear in the first draft and making sure they are clear in the second.
Writing Tweaks	Fixing silly grammar mistakes and make the draft read better off of the criticism I was given.

End of Class Check-In

How have you grown as a writer and researcher since the first day of class?

I honestly don't even know where to start. Before this class I hadn't done this kind of in-depth research before, and it was absolutely terrifying and overwhelming. Now, I have a full literature review, and I feel very confident in my research abililties. I feel like I've become a much more professional, organized writer and am able to express my thoughts in a more comprehensible way.

Where do you still see areas for improvement in your writing and research?

I think it's mostly continuing to get comfortable with organizing and phrasing things so they make the most sense and sound the best. I think this will come with time and practice.

Appendix I: Peer Review of Writing

Response-Centered Peer Review

Answer the following questions and share your answers with your peer.

Introduction
1. Does the introduction effectively describe the research scenario?
2. Does the introduction discuss the research question and the importance of the question?
3. What was effective?
4. What was ineffective?

Literature Review
1. Does the author present at least three themes?
2. Does each theme have at least three supporting articles?
3. Does the author provide at least two direct quotes in this section?
4. Does the author use correct in-text citations?
5. Does the evidence provided support the theme?
6. What was effective?
7. What was ineffective?

Conclusion/Discussion
1. Does the author answer the research question?
2. Does the author discuss how they reached the answer to their question?
3. Does the author discuss future research needed on this topic?
4. What was effective?
5. What was ineffective?

Advice-Centered Peer Review

1. Read your partner's paper and write advice on the paper.

    a) Where are you confused?

    b) Where do you think the author makes a good point?

    c) Where do you feel the author needs more information?

    d) Circle any APA mistakes

    e) Apply the paper rubric

2. Discuss your comments with your partner.

BIBLIOGRAPHY

Aasand, Hardin L., Stevens Amidon, and Debrah Huffman. "Slouching Toward Assessment: One Department's Journey toward Accountability Bliss." In *Coming to Terms with Student Outcomes Assessment: Faculty and Administrators' Journeys to Integrating Assessment in their Work and Institutional Culture*, edited by Peggy L. Maki, 107-122. Sterling, VA: Stylus Publishing, 2010.

Accardi, Maria T. *Feminist Pedagogy for Library Instruction*. Sacramento CA: Library Juice Press, 2013.

———. "Teaching Against the Grain: Critical Assessment in the Library Classroom." In *Critical Library Instruction: Theories and Methods*, edited by Maria T. Accardi, Emily Drabinski, and Alana Kumbier, 251-64. Duluth, MN: Library Juice Press, 2010.

Accardi, Maria T., Emily Drabinski, and Alana Kumbier. *Critical Library Instruction: Theories and Methods*. Duluth, MN: Library Juice Press, 2010.

Accardi, Maria T., and Michelle Reale. "Critical Reflection to Improve and Grow as Librarians Who Teach." Webinar presented for ALAConnect, June 2, 2017. https://www.youtube.com/watch?v=8rzfl6qbFh0&feature=youtu.be.

Alabi, Jaena, and William H. Weare, Jr. "Peer Review of Teaching: Best Practices for a Non-Programmatic Approach." *Communications in Information Literacy* 8, no. 2 (2014): 180-191. https://doi.org/10.15760/comminfolit.2014.8.2.171.

Allen, Mary J. *Assessing Academic Programs in Higher Education.* Bolton, MA: Anker Publishing Company, 2004.

Angelo, Thomas A., and K. Patricia Cross. *Classroom Assessment Techniques.* 2nd ed. San Francisco: Jossey-Bass, 1993.

Ash, Sarah L., Patti H. Clayton, and Maxine P. Atkinson. "Integrating Reflection and Assessment to Capture and Improve Student Learning." *Michigan Journal of Community Service Learning* 11, no. 2 (2005). http://hdl.handle.net/2027/spo.3239521.0011.204.

Association of College and Research Libraries. "Framework for Information Literacy for Higher Education." Adopted January 11, 2016. http://www.ala.org/acrl/standards/ilframework.

Bain, Jennifer. "Integrating Student Voice: Assessment for Empowerment." *Practitioner Research in Higher Education* 4, no. 1 (2010): 14-29.

Bambino, Deborah. "Critical Friends." *Educational Leadership* 59, no. 6 (2002): 25-27.

Beatty, Joshua. "Reading Freire for First-World Librarians." Paper presented at the Annual Conference of the Canadian Association of Professional Academic Librarians, University of Ottawa, Ottawa, ON, May 2015.

Belanger, Jackie, Rebecca Bliquez, and Sharleen Mondal. "Developing a Collaborative Faculty-Librarian Information Literacy Assessment Project." *Library Review 61*, no. 2 (2012): 68-91. https://doi.org/10.1108/00242531211220726.

Boud, David. "Assessment and the Promotion of Academic Values." *Studies in Higher Education* 15, no. 1 (1990): 101-111. https://doi.org/10.1080/03075079012331377621.

———. *Implementing Student Self-Assessment.* Cambelltown, N.S.W.: Higher Education & Development Society of Australasia, 1991.

———. "The Role of Self-Assessment in Student Grading." *Studies in Higher Education* 14, no. 1 (1989): 20-30. https://doi.org/10.1080/0260293890140103.

Boud. David, Ruth Cohen, and Jane Sampson. "Peer Learning and Assessment." *Assessment & Evaluation in Higher Education* 24, no. 4 (1999): 413-426. https://doi.org/10.1080/0260293990240405.

Brew, Christine, and Philip Riley. "Measuring Student Support for Participative Assessment and Related Strategies: Development and Testing of the Beliefs about Participative Assessment Instrument (BAPAI)." *Australian Journal of Teacher Education* 36, no. 4 (2011): 33-52. https://doi.org/10.14221/ajte.2011v36n4.4.

Cook-Sather, Alison, Catherine Bovill, and Peter Felten. *Engaging Students as Partners in Learning and Teaching: A Guide for Faculty.* San Francisco: Josey-Bass, 2014.

Costa, Arthur L., and Bena Kallick. "Through the Lens of a Critical Friend." *Educational Leadership* 51, no. 2 (1993): 49-51.

Couldry, Nick. "Rethinking the Politics of Voice." *Continuum: Journal of Media and Cultural Studies* 23, no. 4 (2009): 579-582. https://doi.org/10.1080/10304310903026594.

Critten, Jessica. Introduction to *Critical Information Literacy: Foundations, Inspiration, and Ideas,* by Annie Downey, 1-10. Sacramento, CA: Library Juice Press, 2016.

Danowitz, Mary Ann and Frank Tuitt, "Enacting Inclusivity through Engaged Pedagogy: A Higher Education Perspective," *Equity & Excellence in Education* 44, no. 1 (2011): 40-56.

Dewey, John. *Democracy and Education: An Introduction to the Philosophy of Education.* New York: Macmillan, 1916.

Dineen, Rachel, and Lyda McCartin. "An Unfinished Journey: Becoming Critical Educators." In *Credit-Bearing Information Literacy Courses: Critical Approaches,* edited by Jessica Critten and Angela Pashia.

Chicago: Association of College and Research Libraries, forthcoming.

Dochy, Filip, M. Segers, and D. Sluijsmans. "The Use of Self-, Peer and Co-Assessment in Higher Education: A Review." *Studies in Higher Education* 21, no. 3 (1999): 331-350. https://doi.org/10.1 080/03075079912331379935.

Downey, Annie. *Critical Information Literacy: Foundations, Inspirations, and Ideas.* Sacramento, CA: Library Juice Press, 2016.

Dutko, Myra. "I Matter, As Does the World: Critical Consciousness in Higher Education." PhD Diss., National Louis University, 2016. http://digitalcommons.nl.edu/cgi/viewcontent. cgi?article=1186&context=diss.

Elmborg, James. "Critical Information Literacy: Definitions and Challenges." In *Transforming Information Literacy Programs: Intersecting Frontiers of Self, Library Culture, and Campus Community*, edited by Carroll Wetzel Wilkinson and Courtney Bruch. Chicago: Association of College and Research Libraries, 2012.

Ellsworth, Elizabeth. "Why Doesn't This Feel Empowering? Working Through the Repressive Myths of Critical Pedagogy." *Harvard Educational Review* 59, no. 3 (1989): 297-325. https://doi. org/10.17763/haer.59.3.058342114k266250.

Erlinger, Allison. "Outcomes Assessment in Undergraduate Information Literacy Instruction: A Systematic Review", *College & Research Libraries* 79, no. 4 (2018): 442-479.

Ewell, Peter. "Assessment, Accountability, and Improvement: Revising the Tension." Occasional Paper #1 presented at the National Institute for Learning Outcomes Assessment (NILOA), University of Illinois and Indiana University, Urbana, IL, November 2009. http://www.learningoutcomeassessment.org/ documents/PeterEwell_005.pdf.

Falchikov, Nancy, and Judy Goldfinch. "Student Peer Assessment in Higher Education: A Meta-Analysis Comparing Peer and

130

Teacher Marks." *Review of Educational Research* 70, no. 3 (2000): 287-322. https://doi.org/10.2307/1170785.

Farkas, Meredith. "Accountability vs. Improvement: Seeking Balance in the Value of Academic Libraries Initiative." *OLA Quarterly* 19, no. 1 (2013): 4-7. https://doi.org/10.7710/1093-7374.1378.

———. "Building and Sustaining a Culture of Assessment: Best Practices for Change Leadership." *Reference Services Review* 41, no. 1 (2013): 13-31. https://doi.org/10.1108/00907321311300857.

Farkas, Meredith G., Lisa J. Hinchliffe, and Amy H. Houk. "Bridges and Barriers: Factors Influencing a Culture of Assessment in Academic Libraries." *College & Research Libraries* 76, no. 2 (2015): 150-169. https://doi.org/10.5860/crl.76.2.150.

Farkas, Meredith G., and Lisa J. Hinchliffe. "Library Faculty and Instructional Assessment: Creating a Culture of Assessment through the High-Performance Programming Model of Organizational Transformation." *Collaborative Librarianship* 5, no. 3 (2013): 177-188.

Feenstra, Kyle. "The process is the Outcome: A Framework for Student 'Research as Praxis.'" Presentation at Librarians' Information Literacy Annual Conference, Liverpool, UK, April 2018. https://www.slideshare.net/infolit_group/the-process-is-the-outcome-a-framework-for-student-research-as-praxis-feenstra.

Fielding, Michael. "Radical Collegiality: Affirming Teaching as an Inclusive Professional Practice." *Australian Educational Researcher* 26, no. 2 (1999): 1-34. https://doi.org/10.1007/bf03219692.

———. "Transformative Approaches to Student Voice: Theoretical Underpinnings, Recalcitrant Realities." *British Educational Research Journal* 30, no. 2 (2004): 295-311. https://doi.org/10.1080/0141192042000195236.

Finley, Priscilla, Susie Skarl, Jennifer Cox, and Diane VanderPol. "Enhancing Library Instruction with Peer Planning."

Reference Services Review 33, no. 1 (2005): 112-122. https://doi. org/10.1108/00907320510581423.

Fisher, Zoe. "Learning is Not a Service." Presentation at the Library Assessments and Metrics Workshop. Colorado Academic Library Association, Denver, CO, November, 2016. https:// quickaskzoe.com/speaking/.

Fluk, Louise R. "Foregrounding the Research Log in Information Literacy Instruction." *Journal of Academic Librarianship*, 41 (2015): 488-498. https://doi.org/10.1016/j.acalib.2015.06.010.

Foley, Jennifer. "Using Feminist Pedagogy to Create Meaningful Assessment for Learning in One-Shot Library Sessions." Presentation at the Southeastern Library Assessment Conference, Atlanta, GA, November 2017. https://scholarworks.gsu.edu/cgi/viewcontent. cgi?article=1049&context=southeasternlac.

Forrest, Margaret E.S. "Learning and Teaching in Action: On Becoming a Critically Reflective Teacher." *Health Information and Libraries Journal* 25, no. 3 (2008): 229-232. https://doi.org/10.1111/ j.1471-1842.2008.00787.x.

Freire, Paulo. *Pedagogy of the Oppressed.* 20th Anniversary ed. New York: Continuum, 1993.

Freire, Paulo and Donaldo P. Macedo, "A Dialogue: Culture, Language, and Race," In *Breaking Free: The Transformative Power of Critical Pedagogy*, edited by Pepi Leistyna, Arlie Woodrum, and Stephen A. Sherblom, 199-228. Cambridge: Harvard Education Review, 1996.

Gardner, Carolyn Caffrey, and Rebecca Halpern. "At Odds with Assessment: Being a Critical Educator within the Academy." In *Critical Library Pedagogy Handbook, Volume 1*, edited by Nicole Pagowsky and Kelly McElroy, 41-51. Chicago: Association of College and Research Libraries, 2016.

Giroux, Henry A. "Teacher Education and Democratic Schooling." In *The Critical Pedagogy Reader*, edited by Antonia Darder, Marta P. Baltodano, and Rodolfo D. Torres, 438-459. New York: Routledge, 2009.

Goodsett, Mandi. "Reflective Teaching: Improving Library Instruction through Self-Reflection." *The Southeastern Librarian* 62, no. 3 (2014): 12-15.

Grant, Maria J. "The Role of Reflection in the Library and Information Sector: A Systematic Review." *Health Information & Libraries Journal* 24, no. 3 (2007): 155-166. https://doi.org/10.1111/j.1471-1842.2007.00731.x.

Graf, Anne Jumonville and Benjamin R. Harris, "Reflective Assessment: Opportunities and Challenges," *Reference Services Review*, 44 (2016): 38-47. https://doi.org/10.1108/rsr-06-2015-0027.

Gregory, Lua, and Shana Higgins. *Information Literacy and Social Justice: Radical Professional Praxis*. Sacramento, CA: Library Juice Press, 2013.

———. "Reorienting an Information Literacy Program Toward Social Justice: Mapping the Core Values of Librarianship to the ACRL Framework." *Communications in Information Literacy* 11, no. 1 (2017): 42-54. https://doi.org/10.15760/comminfolit.2017.11.1.46.

Harris, Benjamin, and Anne Jumonville. "Assessment is Dead, Long Live Assessment: Considering the Risks of Engaged Critical Pedagogy." Paper presented at the Annual Conference of the Canadian Association of Professional Academic Librarians, University of Ottawa, Ottawa, ON, May 2015.

Hay, David, and Ian Kinchin. "Using Concept Mapping to Measure Learning Quality." *Education + Training* 50, no. 2 (2008): 167-182. https://doi.org/10.1108/00400910810862146.

Heron, John. "Assessment Revisited." In _Developing Student Autonomy in Learning,_ edited by David Boud, 77-90. London: Kogan Page, 1988.

Hicks, Alison and Caroline Sinkinson. "Reflections on the Retention Narrative: Extending Critical Pedagogy beyond the Classroom." In _Critical Library Pedagogy Handbook, Volume 1,_ edited by Nicole Pagowsky and Kelly McElroy, 171-183. Chicago: Association of College and Research Libraries, 2016.

hooks, bell. _Teaching to Transgress: Education as the Practice of Freedom._ New York: Routledge, 1994.

Internet Encyclopedia of Philosophy. "Paulo Freire." Accessed May 30, 2018. https://www.iep.utm.edu/freire/.

Jacobs, Heidi. "Information Literacy and Reflective Pedagogical Practice." _The Journal of Academic Librarianship_ 34, no. 3 (2008): 256-262. https://doi.org/10.1016/j.acalib.2008.03.009.

Jones, Steven. _Using Reflection for Assessment._ Iowa City, IA: The University of Iowa Division of Student Life, n.d. https://vp.studentlife.uiowa.edu/assets/Using-Reflection-for-Assessment.pdf.

Kahl, D. H. Jr. "Critical Communication Pedagogy and Assessment: Reconciling Two Seemingly Incongruous Ideas." _International Journal of Communication_ 7, no. 1 (2013): 2610-2630.

Kaufmann, Jodi Jan. "The Practice of Dialogue in Critical Pedagogy." _Adult Education Quarterly: A Journal of Research and Theory_ 60, no. 5 (2010): 456-458. https://doi.org/10.1177/0741713610363021.

Keesing-Styles, Linda. "The Relationship between Critical Pedagogy and Assessment in Teacher Education," _Radical Pedagogy_ 5, no. 1 (2003).

Kincheloe, Joe. _Critical Pedagogy Primer._ 2nd ed. New York: Peter Lang Publishing, 2004.

Kishimoto, Kyoko. "Anti-Racist Pedagogy: From Faculty's Self-Reflection to Organizing within and Beyond the Classroom." _Race Ethnicity_ *and Education*, 21, no. 4 (2016): 540-554. https://doi.org/10.108 0/13613324.2016.1248824.

Krueger, Richard A., and Mary Anne Casey. *Focus Groups: A Practical Guide for Applied Research*. 3rd ed. Thousand Oaks, CA: Sage Publications, 2000.

Larrivee, Barbara. "Transforming Teaching Practice: Becoming the Critically Reflective Teacher." *Reflective Practice* 1, no. 3 (2000): 293-307. https://doi.org/10.1080/713693162.

Levene, Lee-Allision and Polly Frank, "Peer Coaching: Professional Growth and Development for Instruction Librarians." *Reference Services Review* 21, no. 3 (1993): 35-42. https://doi.org/10.1108/ eb049192.

Lorente-Catalán, Eloísa, and David Kirk. "Making the Case for Democratic Assessment Practices within a Critical Pedagogy of Physical Education Teacher Education." *European Physical Education Review* 20, no. 1 (2014): 104-119. https://doi. org/10.1177/1356336x13496004.

Maki, Peggy, L. *Assessing for Learning: Building a Sustainable Commitment Across the*

Institution. Sterling, VA: Stylus Publishing, 2004.

Maki, Peggy L. *Coming to Terms with Student Outcomes Assessment: Faculty and Administrators' Journeys to Integrating Assessment in their Work and Institutional Culture*. Sterling, VA: Stylus Publishing, 2010.

Markowski, Brianne. "Reflecting on the Research Process: Assessing Student Learning with Pre- and Post-Concept Maps." Presention at the LOEX Annual Conference, Houston, TX, 2018.

Martin, Graham A., and Jeremy M. Double. "Developing Higher Education Teaching Skills through Peer Observation and Collaborative Reflection." *Innovations in Education &*

Training International 35, no. 2 (1998): 161-170. https://doi. org/10.1080/1355800980350210.

McCullagh, John F. "How Can Video Supported Reflection Enhance Teachers' Professional Development?" *Cultural Studies of Science Education* 7, no. 1 (2012): 137-152. https://doi.org/10.1007/ s11422-012-9396-0.

McGuinness, Claire, and Michelle Brien. "Using Reflective Journals to Assess the Research Process." *Reference Services Review* 35, no. 1 (2007): 21-40. https://doi.org/10.1108/00907320710729346.

McLaren, Peter. *Life in Schools.* 6th ed. Boulder: Paradigm Publishers, 2015.

McLeod, Julie. "Student Voice and the Politics of Listening in Higher Education." *Critical Studies in Education* 52, no. 2 (2011): 179-189. https://doi.org/10.1080/17508487.2011.572830.

Moon, Jennifer. *A Handbook of Reflective and Experiential Learning: Theory and Practice.* London: Routledge, 2004.

Moon, Jennifer. *Learning Journals: A Handbook for Reflective Practice and Professional Development.* 2nd ed. London: Routledge, 2006.

Musil, Caryn McTighe, ed. *Students at the Center: Feminist Assessment.* Washington, D.C.: Association of American Colleges, 1992.

Norbury, Linda. "Peer Observation of Teaching: A Method for Improving Teaching Quality." *New Review of Academic Librarianship* 7, no. 1 (2001): 87-99. https://doi. org/10.1080/13614530109516823.

Nulty, Duncan D. "Peer and Self-Assessment in the First Year of University." *Assessment & Evaluation in Higher Education* 36, no. 5 (2011): 493-507. https://doi.org/10.1080/02602930903540983.

Oakleaf, Megan. "The Information Literacy Instruction Assessment Cycle: A Guide for Increasing Student Learning and Improving Librarian Instructional Skills." *Journal of Documentation* 65, no. 4 (2009): 539-560. https://doi.org/10.1108/00220410910970249.

———. "What's the Value of an Academic Library? The Development of the ACRL Value of Academic Libraries Comprehensive Research Review and Report." *Australian Academic & Research Libraries* 42, no. 1 (2011): 1-13. https://doi.org/10.1080/00048623.2011.10722200.

O'Connor, Catherine and Sarah Michaels, "When is Dialogue 'Dialogic'?." *Human Development* 50 (2007): 275-285. doi:10.1159/000106415.

Oravitz, Michael, Kristin Bovaird-Abbo, and Karen Hessler. "Just Ask: Enriching Evaluation through Face-to-Face Student Feedback." Presentation at the Center for Enhancement of Teaching and Learning, University of Northern Colorado, Greeley, CO, 2015.

Özek, Yvonne Hultman, Gudrun Edgren, and Katarina Jandér. "Implementing the Critical Friend Method for Peer Feedback among Teaching Librarians in an Academic Setting." *Evidence Based Library and Information Practice* 7, no. 4 (2012): 68-81. https://doi.org/10.18438/b81c8w.

Pagowsky, Nicole, and Kelly McElroy, eds. *Critical Library Pedagogy Handbook*. Chicago: Association of College and Research Libraries, 2016.

Palomba, Catherine A., and Trudy W. Banta. *Assessment Essentials: Planning, Implementing, and Improving Assessment in Higher Education*. San Francisco: Jossey-Bass Publishers, 1999.

Pavlovich, Kathryn. "The Development of Reflective Practice through Student Journals." *Higher Education Research & Development* 26, no. 3 (2007): 281-295. https://doi.org/10.1080/07294360701494302.

Peterson, Elizabeth. "Problem-Based Learning as Teaching Strategy." In *Critical Library Instruction: Theories and Method*, edited by Maria T. Accardi, Emily Drabinski, and Alana Kumbier, 71-80. Duluth, MN: Library Juice Press, 2010.

Pope, Nigel K. Ll. "The Impact of Stress in Self- and Peer Assessment." *Assessment & Evaluation in Higher Education* 30, no. 1 (2005): 51-63. https://doi.org/10.1080/0260293042003243896.

Radcliff, Carolyn J., Mary Lee Jensen, Joseph A. Salem Jr., Kenneth J. Burhanna, and Julie A. Gedeon. *A Practical Guide to Information Literacy Assessment for Academic Librarians.* Westport, CT.: Libraries Unlimited, 2007.

Reale, Michelle. *Becoming a Reflective Librarian and Teacher: Strategies for Mindful Academic Practice.* Chicago: ALA Editions, 2017.

Reynolds, Michael, and Kiran Trehan. "Assessment: A Critical Perspective." *Studies in Higher Education* 25, no. 3 (2000): 267-278. https://doi.org/10.1080/03075070050193406.

Robinson, Carol, and Carol Taylor. "Theorizing Student Voice: Values and Perspectives." *Improving Schools* 10, no. 1 (2007): 5-17. https://doi.org/10.1177/1365480207073702.

Rosaen, Cheryl L., Mary Lundeberg, Marjorie Cooper, Anny Fritzen, and Marjorie Terpstra. "Noticing Noticing: How does Investigation of Video Records Change How Teachers Reflect on their Experiences?" *Journal of Teacher Education* 59, no. 4 (2008): 347-360. https://doi.org/10.1177/0022487108322128.

Samson, Sue, and Donna E. McCrea. "Using Peer Review to Foster Good Teaching." *Reference Services Review* 36, no. 1 (2008): 61-70. https://doi.org/10.1108/00907320810852032.

Schniedewind, Nancy. "Teaching Feminist Process." *Women's Studies Quarterly* 15, no. 3/4 (1987): 15-31.

Schroeder, Robert. *Critical Journeys: How 14 Librarians Came to Embrace Critical Practice.* Sacramento: Library Juice Press, 2014.

Seale, Jane. "Doing Student Voice Work in Higher Education: An Exploration of the Value of Participatory Methods." *British Educational Research Journal* 36, no. 6 (2010): 995-1015. https://doi.org/10.1080/01411920903342038.

Shapiro, Joan Poliner. "What is Feminist Assessment?" In *Students at the Center: Feminist Assessment*, edited by Caryn McTighe Musil, 29-38. Washington, D.C.: Association of American Colleges, 1992.

Shor, Ira. *Empowering Education: Critical Teaching for Social Change*. Chicago: University of Chicago Press, 1992.

———. *When Students Have Power: Negotiating Authority in a Critical Pedagogy*. Chicago: The University of Chicago Press, 1996.

Shor, Ira, and Paulo Freire. *A Pedagogy for Liberation: Dialogues on Transforming Education*. South Hadley, MA: Bergin & Garvey, 1987.

Siddiqui, Zarrin Seema, Diana Jonas-Dwyer, and Sandra E. Carr. "Twelve Tips for Peer Observation of Teaching." *Medical Teacher* 29, no. 4 (2007): 297-300. https://doi.org/10.1080/01421590701291451.

Sinkinson, Caroline. "An Assessment of Peer Coaching to Drive Professional Development and Reflective Teaching." *Communications in Information Literacy* 5, no. 1 (2011): 9-20. https://doi.org/10.15760/comminfolit.2011.5.1.99.

Snavely, Loanne, and Nancy Dewald. "Developing and Implementing Peer Review of Academic Librarians' Teaching: An Overview and Case Report." *Journal of Academic Librarianship* 37, no. 4 (2011): 343-351. https://doi.org/10.1016/j.acalib.2011.04.009.

Stewart, Saran. "Everything in Di Dark Muss Come to Light: A Postcolonial Investigation of the Practice of Extra Lessons at the Secondary Level in Jamaica's Education System." PhD Diss., University of Denver, 2013. ProQuest Dissertations Publishing.

Stewart, Saran. "Advancing a Critical and Inclusive Praxis: Pedagogical Curriculum Innovations for Social Change in the Caribbean." In *Race, Equity and the Learning Environment: The Global Relevance of Critical and Inclusive Pedagogies in Higher Education*, edited by Frank Tuitt, Chayla Haynes, and Saran Stewart, 9-22. Sterling, VA: Stylus Publishing, 2016.

Sullivan, Peter B., Alexandra Buckle, Gregg Nicky, and Sarah H. Atkinson. "Peer Observation of Teaching as a Faculty Development Tool." *BMC Medical Education* 12, no. 1 (2012): 26. https://doi.org/10.1186/1472-6920-12-26.

Swanson, Troy A. "Applying a Critical Pedagogical Perspective to Information Literacy Standards." *Community & Junior College Libraries* 12, no. 4 (2005): 65-77. https://doi.org/10.1300/j107v12n04_08.

Tan, Kelvin H. K. "Does Student Self-Assessment Empower or Discipline Students?" *Assessment & Evaluation in Higher Education* 29, no. 6 (2004): 651-662. https://doi.org/10.1080/026029304 2000227209.

Taylor, Terry, Joan Arth, Amy Solomon, and Naomi Williamson. *100% Information Literacy Success*. Clifton Park, NY: Thomson Delmar Learning, 2007.

Tewell, Eamon. "A Decade of Critical Information Literacy: A Review of the Literature." *Communications in Information Literacy* 9, no. 1 (2015): 24-43. https://doi.org/10.15760/comminfolit.2015.9.1.174.

———. "The Problem with Grit: Dismantling Deficit Models in Information Literacy Instruction," Presentation at the LOEX Annual Conference, Houston, TX, May 5, 2018. http://www.loexconference.org/sessions.html#Tewell.

———. "The Practice and Promise of Critical Information Literacy: Academic Librarians' Involvement in Critical Information Literacy." *College & Research Libraries* 79, no. 1 (2018):10-34.

Tompkins, Elizabeth K. "A Reflective Teaching Journal: An Instructional Improvement Tool for Academic Librarians." *College & Undergraduate Libraries* 16, no. 4 (2009): 221-238. https://doi.org/10.1080/10691310903355937.

Tristán, Jose María Barroso. "Henry Giroux: The Necessity of Critical Pedagogy in Dark Times." *Truth Out*, February 6, 2013. http://

www.truth-out.org/news/item/14331-a-critical-interview-with-henry-giroux.

Tuitt, Frank. "Afterword: Realizing a More Inclusive Pedagogy." In *Race and Higher Education: Rethinking Pedagogy in Diverse College Classrooms* edited by Annie Howell and Frank Tuitt, 243-268. Cambridge, MA: Harvard Education Publishing Group, 2003.

Tuitt, Frank, Chayla Haynes, and Saran Stewart. *Race, Equity and the Learning Environment: The Global Relevance of Critical and Inclusive Pedagogies in Higher Education.* Sterling, VA: Stylus Publishing, 2016.

Turabian, Kate L., Gregory G. Colomb, and Joseph M. Williams. *Student's Guide to Writing College Papers.* Chicago Guides to Writing, Editing, and Publishing. 4th ed. Chicago: The University of Chicago Press, 2010.

Vidmar, Dale J. "Reflective Peer Coaching: Crafting Collaborative Self-Assessment in Teaching." *Research Strategies* 20, no. 3 (2005): 135-148. https://doi.org/10.1016/j.resstr.2006.06.002.

Weaver, Kari, and Michelle Petrie. "Sociology in Action: A Comparative Study of Embedded Interventions for Improved Research and Writing in the Introduction of Sociological Research Methods." Presented at Librarians' Information Literacy Annual Conference, Liverpool, UK, April 2018. https://www.slideshare.net/infolit_group/sociology-in-action-a-comparative-study-of-embedded-interventions-for-improved-research-and-writing-in-the-introduction-of-sociological-research-methods-weaver-petrie

Wink, Joan. *Critical Pedagogy: Notes from the Real World.* 2nd ed. New York: Longman, 2000

York-Barr, Jennifer, William A. Sommers, Gail S. Ghere, and Jo Montie. *Reflective Practice to Improve Schools: An Action Guide for Educators.* Thousand Oaks, CA: Corwin Press, 2001.

About the Authors

Lyda Fontes McCartin is a Professor and Head of Information Literacy and Undergraduate Support at the University of Northern Colorado. She leads a team of innovative librarians who are recognized as an ACRL Information Literacy Best Practices Exemplary Program in Pedagogy. Lyda earned her MA in History and her MLIS from the University of Alabama in Tuscaloosa. She currently serves as UNC's Senior Faculty Assessment Fellow; in this role she provides consultation, guidance, and professional development on course and program-level assessment of student learning to faculty across campus. She has presented on assessment of student learning at state, national, and international conferences. Her current research agenda includes critical information literacy, critical assessment, and assessment of information literacy.

Rachel Dineen is an Assistant Professor in Information Literacy and Undergraduate Support at the University of Northern Colorado. She currently teaches credit-bearing information literacy classes at the undergraduate level. Rachel earned her MS in Library and Information Science from the University of Illinois, Urbana-Champaign. Her research interests include critical information literacy, feminist pedagogy, assessment, and art and design librarianship.

INDEX

CPSIA information can be obtained
at www.ICGtesting.com
Printed in the USA
BVHW040828270820
587456BV00013B/390

9 781634 000352